SIGMA RISING

A novel by
JOHN RANDOLPH PRICE

SIGMA RISING
By John Randolph Price

In the year 2021, twelve men and women in high government posts suddenly disappear. When it is realized that the spouses are also missing, the FBI launches a multi-pronged investigation along with a complete media blackout.

Kidnapping by a foreign terrorist group is suspected, but when it is realized that there were no witnesses, signs of struggle, or evidence of foul play, intelligence services consider the possibility that the group left of their own accord and now represent a threat to our national security.

Keri Winslow, a Washington television reporter, and Phillip Lansing, White House correspondent for a major network, discover the location of the missing VIPs and are soon involved in the unraveling of an ancient mystery that has been fearfully controversial for centuries--that there are those among us who are not of this world.

The characters in *Sigma Rising* are strong and memorable as they move through the twists and turns of a frenzied nation, clandestine meetings, paranormal experiences, grief and new found love, and a greater understanding about life and death.

The secrets of the benevolent beings who have been active on Earth for two million years is finally revealed. Although based on the spiritual truth of

Ancient Wisdom with valid insights on the meaning of illusion and reality, this is basically a work of fiction. Names, characters, places and incidents are the product of the author's imagination.

***

This novel is dedicated to the love of my life, Jan Price, who knows that there are many worlds of living reality in the superuniverse of heavenly creation.

Chapter 1

The large black sedan stopped at the South Gate of the White House, the driver's window lowered part way. The marine guard peered inside, stepped back and saluted. The driver nodded and continued through the cold misty rain to the West Wing.

In his early sixties, tall, well-built, with pale blue eyes and brownish gray hair, FBI Director Wallace Edward Brent was not looking forward to the meeting in the Oval Office. He had been awake most of the night searching for answers, reasons, motives, *anything* he could tell the president that would make sense. He had come up with nothing, not even wildly imaginative scenarios involving the lunatic fringe. Brent felt helpless. He was known for his hands-on command and quick-strike actions in solving more than a dozen crimes of domestic terrorism. He didn't like the raw sense of futility gripping him this early morning.

A secretary announced his arrival. As he entered the Oval Office the president gave him a quick glance of acknowledgement and returned to the morning paper, turning the pages for any news related to the director's visit. "Be with you in a moment, Wallace."

Brent removed his topcoat and sat on the sofa to the right of the president's desk, waited for him to complete the scan, wondering why the first lady didn't advise him on how to dress for power. His gray suit was ill-fitting, the top of the coat hanging back two fingers from his blue shirt collar, and the blue and tan stripped tie loosened at the neck decidedly inappropriate. Brent suspected he was wearing the usual heel-worn loafers.

Director Brent prided himself on being a meticulous dresser: smart, stylish, well-groomed. Quite a difference, he thought, including their backgrounds. Brent was a west Texas rancher's son who deserted his boots, straw hat, and dust-in-the-mouth heritage to study law at Harvard, later becoming an FBI special agent and competitively maneuvering his way to the top of the Bureau. Despite his uneasiness at the moment, he knew the job as though it was created for him.

The president, a city boy governing the most powerful nation on earth, seemed more like a back-country tourist who had stopped by the White House for a visit. Brent could see him cast in a movie as a small town high school coach selling life insurance on the side to make extra money. The ironies in life amused him.

The president folded the paper. "All right Wallace, let's hear what you have."

"Mr. President, I appreciate you seeing me before the others arrive. They've all got to be a bit apprehensive. I admit I am, and I thought that maybe together we could assuage the anxiety and get a productive forum going."

President Samual Underwood looked up, shook his head. "This isn't something that makes me strut with confidence either. I've cancelled two off-premise meetings today. Wallace, there has got to be a logical explanation for what's happened."

The FBI man rubbed the back of his neck. "Logical does not mean benign, Mr. President. Have you read my report?"

"Yes, when I returned last night from the London conference. Vice President Ranston called me yesterday with what he knew, then Bob Evans gave me a summary on the chopper ride from Andrews. I agreed he should call the individuals you requested for the meeting--Ranston, Defense Secretary Pellman, Director Santana of the CIA, NSC's General Lindly. I also asked Evans to attend. I don't know what he told them except that it was an emergency session."

"Your chief of staff shook them up. Secretary Pellman called me last night. He's nervous as hell."

"They are due in less than thirty minutes," the president said as he leaned back in his chair and looked at his watch. "If we're going to calm them down and have a constructive meeting, I've got to have more details."

The FBI Director moved to the edge of the sofa. "As I reported, Mr. President, seven top government people, including two of the Joint Chiefs, have vanished into thin air in the past three days. I've got most of our field offices working on it. Tony Voger is heading up the domestic investigation and Langley has alerted CIA case officers to check sources for any related information on foreign terrorist activities. But right now we're still in the dark. Not a single clue."

The president looked at the report on his desk. "Evans said Ambassador Livingston-Vance was seen at mid-morning leaving the private garage at the UN in her limo. As I understand it, her aide told you the ambassador had been informed her husband was seriously ill, but she never arrived at their home on Long Island."

The director leaned closer. "That was three days ago, and neither the NYPD nor my agents have found any sign of her, the car, the driver, or the person who supposedly gave her the message. Oh, and something else that wasn't in the report. We can't find her husband either. We've checked every hospital in the area, and no one by the name of George Vance has been admitted."

"The FBI was called in because of a possible kidnapping." The director nodded. Massaging his forehead with both hands, the president asked, "But what about the media? Evans said there hadn't been anything on the news, and there was nothing in the paper this morning."

Brent smiled. "We covered that with some crisis management. A party line has been developed for each missing person, with the appropriate people, aides, staff members, and both the New York police and Metropolitan cops here cooperating with us. We'll keep a lid on it as long as we can."

"Good thinking."

"Just hope I covered the bases quickly enough. That same day, Attorney General Ames received a call on his cell phone while having lunch at the Round Robin. The people with him said he listened for a minute, put the phone back in his pocket and excused himself, said he was going to the men's room. He never came back. His wife is also missing. That afternoon Admiral Jessops of the Joint Chiefs was supposed to board a flight at Andrews. He didn't show and hasn't been seen since. I figured we might be involved in a far-reaching conspiracy, so I alerted the Secret Service and beefed up security on the Hill and other appropriate spots. Also closed down the media pipelines. There's probably a lot of rumors going around, but at least we've got a handle on it for now."

The president stood and walked to the window. Light rain had turned to snow. He watched as the lawn and gardens were slowly camouflaged, a patchwork quilt of colors soon to be an unblemished blanket of white feathery crystals.

As a forty-four year old Miami lawyer he had won his first political race and came to Washington as a congressman. Ten years later he was tapped as the ideal number two man in Governor Morris' run for the presidency. Morris had said with Underwood's centrist philosophy, his charisma and Hollywood-handsome looks, he would be the media's darling. Of course Underwood had no idea James Morris would drop dead after only six months in office. Samual Underwood didn't enjoy being the President of the United States, not at this moment. He took a deep breath and turned around to speak to the director.

"Wallace, according to Evans' briefing, the next one to disappear after Admiral Jessops was Senator Obrey, and you say he was having dinner with friends in Georgetown?"

"Yes, the Albrights. That was night before last. Senator Obrey practiced law with Joseph Albright before entering politics. Since Obrey is majority leader, an agent was assigned to go with him and waited outside in the car. Mrs. Albright said she left the senator and Mrs. Obrey alone in the kitchen for a few minutes and when she returned they were gone. The agent saw no one enter or leave the house. We checked the Obrey home--empty-- and his office hasn't heard from him."

The president returned to his chair behind the large desk. "And even with the increased security, Secretary of State Matthews, General Craig, and Justice Ellenberg are also missing."

"Yes, since yesterday afternoon. I thought we had a damn good net in and around State, Justice, the Capitol, the Supreme Court Building and the Pentagon. But it's as though the three of them were seen one moment and gone the next. Vanished. And while I hate to say this, I think we have to consider the possibility that all seven are dead."

The president closed his eyes. "I'd rather think otherwise. Now, other than a government or military connection, what are the common denominators?"

"Our computer analysis came up with four. One, all are what you might consider middle-readers, political moderates and fairly liberal in their religious beliefs. No extremism."

"That would seem to eliminate foreign terrorists. It doesn't seem these people would draw a zealot's attention."

"You may be right, but their mainstream approach could be anathema to hardcore militias and those who might be angered by people perceived as too judicious, too *normal*. To them, if you are not a radical righter you're suspected of treason. You know how they feel about you, particularly after you spoke of freedom as being a higher priority than security. Then your ardent reliance and cooperation with the U.N. to solve international problems caused some negative reactions."

President Underwood nodded. "There are still a few pockets of resistance, some discontents, but Americans are enjoying a sense of peace and plenty once again." He paused, thought for a moment. "Wallace, since the turn of the century this nation--and the world I might add-has gone through difficult times, and we still have much work to do. But we've turned the corner with our focus on government obedience to the people rather than passing more laws to suppress their rights. Believe me when I say that my reorganization of the government has nothing to do with the missing people. Now, what are the other similarities?"

"All are happily married with no children, and in every case the spouse is also missing. And the third coincidence, if there is such a thing, is that four of the seven were adopted."

"I'm assuming you're following through to see if there is any significance to that element."

"Yes sir, we are. Of course, background checks for security clearances don't always make the distinction between natural and legal parents. In the case of the four, the information was volunteered in early bio sketches. But we are initiating new probes into the backgrounds of the others to see if anything turns up."

"Have you found any other top people who were adopted as children?"

"Only one so far, House Speaker Andrews, but we're checking the records of essentially all elected and appointed officials."

"And the other common denominator?"

"Each one came up from nowhere. Obscure one day, bright young stars the next. The latter point is an exaggeration, but I think you know what I mean."

The president nodded. "Secretary Matthews immediately comes to mind. He taught history at a small college in the Northeast, wrote a book on the Arab-Israeli peace process and was recruited by State to serve as a consultant on Middle East affairs. There were a lot of moans in the inner circles when President Morris called him to fill the secretary of state post in the new cabinet, but he's served his country well."

The president shifted in his chair, looked again at his watch. "The others should be arriving shortly. We'll see what we can do to make sense out of this and avoid a national panic."

***

Megan Andrews, wife of House Speaker Julius Andrews, paused in the large living room and looked around. "Up to the bedroom," a voice said, "let's go."

She frowned. *More time*, she wanted to say, to stretch the seconds and relish the moments of their lives in the lovely old Georgetown house. She saw the flowers on the side table by the couch, the camellias laced with baby's breath she had brought home from the florist only the day before. She lifted her eyes to the painting above the fireplace, a print of Monet's *Old St. Lazare Station, Paris*. Was the train arriving or departing? *Probably the latter*, she thought, *like me and Julius. Not yet, please.* Megan was feeling tender, nostalgia sweeping over her. She and Julius had lived in this home for twenty years. Now it was about to be over. *No time for regrets.* She felt a hand on her arm, leading her up the stairs.

***

It was almost noon when the meeting with the president and his advisors was concluded. There had been one interruption. An incoming call reported that four additional senators and the Speaker of the House had suddenly vanished. The president said he would consider all recommendations and that the media blackout would continue. He spent the rest of the day in the residency with his wife Julia.

***

Ambassador Merriam Livingston-Vance paced the small windowless enclosure, counting the stone inlays from one end of the room to the other. She was remembering her first day at school in this country.

Chapter 2

The blue-eyed girl with the flaming red hair and milk-white complexion looked at herself in the full length mirror and sighed. "I do not know what to do with this hair. And these clothes do not feel right. Do you have any suggestions?"

The stocky man in his mid-forties standing beside her said, "You look fine." He placed a gentle hand on her shoulder. "You're a bit taller than average for your age, and clothes won't hide that." He laughed. "Which means all the boys will look up to you." Seeing she wasn't amused, he said, "As for the hair, try a pony tail."

Seven year old Merriam Livingston pulled her hair back and fastened it with a clasp, then turned around and flashed a brief smile. "Shall I call you father?"

"Too formal. Let's use mommy and daddy, and pronounce your words carefully to veil the accent."

"Do not worry. In a short time I will be speaking as a true midwesterner. But you are right. The less notice I attract the better. Being adopted is going to cause enough talk. I am sure your neighbors have spread the word. The children will ask what happened to my real parents. Frankly, I do not want to get into any discussions about my past." She moved around him and sat on the bed to put on her shoes.

He was silent for a moment as he opened the curtains to her bedroom and looked out at the tree-lined street below. A hazy morning, the sun just breaking through. Weather forecast promised the low seventies by afternoon. Turning to her, he said, "School started a week ago, and coming in late you can't help but be the center of attention. But that will quickly pass, and in the meantime I would suggest you be the shy, silent type. If you're asked, just say that you'd rather not talk about your parents, that Charles and Anne Livingston are your family now."

"Did I hear my name mentioned?" Anne asked as she entered the room with a cup of coffee. She was wearing jeans, plaid shirt and sweater, the purse over her shoulder suggesting it was time to take Merriam to school.

"Just talking about handling her first encounter with the kids at school," Charles said. He smiled inwardly at the contrast between the two females. Anne a short-haired, brown-eyed diminutive blonde, and Merriam nearly as tall at seven years old with that shock of bright red hair and deep blue eyes.

Anne finished her last sip of coffee. "I don't see that as being a problem, but I would suggest that you watch and learn from the other children. For example, look at the way you're sitting, Merriam, straight as an arrow. Slump a little. Place your elbow on your knee and rest your head in your hand. Make your body appear lazy."

Merriam followed the directions, said with a grin, "I feel ridiculous. And I guess I should run and skip and chatter breathlessly on the playground, clap my hands frequently. What was it Epictetus said? *Who is not attracted by bright and pleasant children, to prattle, to creep, and to play with them?"*

Anne gave her a playful pat. "Yes, and don't forget to throw in a scream once in a while. Sniffle too. Runny noses are most child-like. Also, Merriam, watch what you say. A few slang words are appropriate. Just listen to how the others are expressing themselves, and don't sound too intelligent for your age."

Merriam stood and tucked the white blouse into the dark green skirt. "I feel as though I am playing a role on stage."

"And so you are," Charles said, a serious look on his face.

Merriam glanced at her watch and took a deep breath. "I guess it is time to go."

***

"Children," Mrs. Renfro said in a loud voice to break through the buzz of conversation and ripples of giggles, "take your seats now and be very quiet. We have a new student joining us today. Her name is Merriam Livingston, and I'm sure each one of you will make her feel welcome. Merriam, please stand and say hello to your classmates."

Merriam stood and nodded with a shy smile, then quickly sat down, feeling all eyes on her.

Mrs. Renfro said, "When we go out for recess, children, I want all of you to introduce yourselves to Merriam. She just moved to town, and I'm sure she's looking forward to making new friends."

The little blonde haired boy behind Merriam touched her shoulder and whispered, "My name's Bobby and my daddy's a policeman and carries a gun."

She turned back toward him, said, "My father owns

a book store. When you are older you might enjoy browsing the shelves."

Bobby fell back in his seat, eyes squinting.

Merriam smiled to herself, then focused on what Mrs. Renfro was writing on the blackboard.

* * *

Charles Livingston picked up the ringing phone at his store. Hearing the voice he put the caller on hold and went into his private office and closed the door, quickly moving to the phone on his desk. He said, "I was expecting your call earlier. Anne took Merriam to school this morning, and by now I imagine she's settling in without difficulty. How about the others?"

A woman's voice on the other end said, "I have reports from ten of the twelve, and everything seems to be in order. I'll check on Carlton Matthews next." She paused. "Just remember, Charles, everything from home life, to school, and all regular childhood activities must appear as normal as possible."

"What about church?"

"Do what is socially accepted and go where the three of you would be most comfortable, probably one with a large congregation where you would blend in yet still be seen. You don't want to be singled out for participation in informal church gatherings."

"How often do you wish us to report to you?"

"As I've told the others, once a month for a year, then annually. Once Merriam leaves home to attend college, she's on her own, and you and Anne will have no further responsibility."

"I'll call you a month from today," Charles said as he turned the calendar and marked the date with the letter 'A'.

***

Although she was viewed by the other children as strange, shy, an egghead, and hesitant to join in games, she went through the school year without incident. It was spring, however, before she made any real friends. Debbie Nelson, one of the most popular girls in school, invited her over for a slumber party. From then on Merriam was accepted as part of the inner circle of Highlands Elementary School. She was beginning to enjoy the role of a typical youngster from an average American family.

The following summer while returning home from an outing on Lake Michigan, eight year old Merriam told her parents she wanted to have a birthday party. "Before school starts in September," she said from the back seat.

Charles moved to another lane to get away from a tail-gating eighteen wheeler, said, "Why do I have the feeling that you're not referring to the kind of party that would appeal to most kids your age?"

Merriam laughed. "And guess who I want to invite."

Anne looked back at the beaming child. "You can't be serious. I don't think it's a good idea to get you all together in one place. You might slip and be overheard by someone and--"

"I've already called for approval," Merriam said, brushing the sand off her legs. "It's okay if we meet on the island, but only for a day and a night. The date's been set, the eighteenth of this month."

"On *the* island?" Charles asked.

"Uh huh. The eighteenth is a Saturday. We could go over that day, spend the night, and return home on Sunday. What do you think?"

Anne grinned. "Since you have authorization and it's

all arranged, I think it's a great idea!"

"Me too," Charles said, wishing he had thought of it.

***

The Livingston's arrived at mid-afternoon on the eighteenth, and were sipping iced tea in the large ultra-modern structure at one end of the island when the others appeared. After warm embraces and much chatter, the children put on their bathing suits and left together for a few hours of private time on the beach. The parents smiled approvingly as they watched the nine boys and three girls run through the dense green forest toward the water.

It was a beautiful day, a blue sky holding only the bright afternoon sun, not a cloud in sight, water lapping up on the sand in gentle waves prompted by a passing ferry. Frank Jessops reached the water first and high-stepped until knee deep, then dived under, the other children following. Playing as dolphins, someone might have thought as three boys suddenly burst forth from under water with a teammate balanced on strong shoulders, while the others took great leaps and dives in synchronous movements.

Back on the beach they stretched out on the sand side by side, laughing softly and gazing at the sky. From above, the scene could have been viewed as a canvas painted by a master artist, the children representing faultless specimens of the human family, each one proportionally perfect with exquisite features. *A race of young gods from ancient mythology*, such a painting might have been called.

"Let's make a circle," Carlton Matthews said as he took Merriam's hand. They quickly gathered around and began circling, the ring of happy, dancing children observed by a pleasure boat skimming across the water, the occupants waving, smiling. Faster and faster they ran, the sounds of laughter reaching a crescendo, and then fading as they collapsed on the sand and watched as their dizziness moved sky, sun, and trees in revolving patterns.

They lay there until Robert Ames thought of something else to do: tell each other about their new lives in America. He said, "My biggest problem was getting rid of the accent. It was only when I began to speak as though my nose was stopped up, like other New Yorkers, did people stop asking me where I was from."

"That wasn't my problem," Frank Jessops said as he lifted his long legs skyward. "The most difficult thing for me was to curtail my athletic abilities and appear average, at least to some extent. Many of the kids seem to be so uncoordinated. How about you, Merriam?"

She grinned, leaned over on an elbow. "It's been difficult keeping my mouth shut about the teaching methods being used. They're so crude you wonder how the children ever learn anything." She looked at Lisa Jackson. "What was your biggest hurdle?"

Lisa shook her head and frowned. "Getting used to the food, especially the weekend barbecues. The first time I was served a hot dog, I stared at it for a moment and walked away. My stomach still turns just thinking about it." She laughed. "The Sunday afternoon ritual later included hamburgers, steaks, shish kebabs, and spare ribs, with mostly casseroles served during the week. Mother said I should learn to eat everything so I'd fit in with the other neighborhood kids. I'm trying."

Merriam turned to Curtis O'Conner. The little blonde-haired boy with the tight curls looked away, then said, his voice soft, "I don't know about the rest of you, but I've been feeling lonely. I haven't made many friends and my parents are uncomfortable about me asking someone over to spend the night. All I do is go to school, read, listen to the radio, and wish I was back home. "

Claudia Andrade got up and walked across the circle to where he was sitting. She put her arms around him, said, "Curtis, call me anytime you're lonesome and we'll talk." She reached up and brushed a tear from his eye. "Believe it or not, you may be getting acclimated to conditions here faster than we are. I'm talking about the emotions, the tears. You've tapped into a collective sense of depression, which you can learn how to handle. We still have to do that. Now, if you want to cry, just go ahead and I'll hold you." She pulled the little eight-year-old boy close and let him weep openly. Finally Curtis drew back, rubbing his red eyes. "I'm okay now, feel much better. Thank you."

The other eleven softly clapped their hands, and Merriam said, "Let's go on around the circle. We can learn from each other." When the last one, Simon Ellenberg, had his say, the children discussed how helpful their adoptive parents were, the different local environments in which they were growing up, and their plans for the future. Then they fell silent once more and sat in a line together staring at the water, the late afternoon sun behind them casting warm rays on their beautifully tanned bodies.

Finally, as the sun dropped below the tree line, Carlton Matthews got up and made an imprint of his hand in the wet sand, saying, "May each one of you make your impression on mine, symbolically linking us once more as an unbreakable chain."

"Together as one," spoke each child while pressing a palm into the sandy indentation.

**

The annual reunions on the island continued for several years, with numerous telephone contacts made during the school terms. Even though they lived in various parts of the country, the twelve were never out of touch with each other for long. When a boy asked Claudia Andrade for her first date, she delayed an answer until she could call Curtis O'Connor for advice on what would be expected. Curtis said he didn't know, to ask her parents. Soon the twelve were in coast-to-coast communication with each other on the topic of sex.

Other calls focused on how to handle IQ tests after two of them startled their teachers with supernormal scores, how to overcome periods of being homesick, and more talk about why the American people eat as they do. "It's not so much *what* they eat," Lisa Jackson said to Merriam on the phone from Dallas, "it's how *much* they eat. It is a wonder that everyone is not obese."

They also talked about the civil rights movement, hula-hoops, backyard bomb shelters, Elvis Presley, ridiculous television shows, the Beatles, and rock music.

In the summer of nineteen sixty-three, they applauded the Mercury 9 flight into space the previous May. With L. Gordon Cooper Jr. in the capsule, a 22-orbit endurance record was set while sending back the first TV pictures from space. From the wet sand Frank Jessops and Frederick Craig built a rocket and spacecraft poised for lift-off while others fashioned a large ball of sand to represent the moon.

Curtis O'Connor asked, "How long do you think it

will be before the first astronaut walks on the lunar surface?"

"It will be in this decade," Merriam said, standing on the round mass of sand, "and I bet they land on the Sea of Tranquility."

"Why are they doing this?" Lisa asked. "It's going to cost billions of dollars, and probably some lives, and what will they have to show for their efforts?"

"Rocks from the moon eventually," Carlton Matthews said. "But the bottom line is to push through technological barriers and restructure scientific beliefs. Let them have their moments of glory and we'll celebrate with them. Remember what Shakespeare said, 'knowledge is the wing wherewith we fly to heaven'."

Lisa shook her head. "They're flying the wrong way if they want to get *there.*"

"Have patience, Lisa," Simon Ellenberg said, "they're learning. Maybe one of these days they'll even move past the idea of the absolute existence of matter."

Claudia laughed. "And solve the quantum measurement problem."

"All things are possible," Simon said.

***

In November of that year they were shocked by the assassination of President Kennedy in Dallas. They wondered if their people would someday be mentioned in connection with a government cover-up.

Chapter 3

In the summer of nineteen sixty-five, after graduating from high school, all twelve as valedictorians, the young people came back to the island without their parents. A meeting had been scheduled with the group's director, a time for decisions about their college education and careers. But play came first for the teenagers.

They built a bonfire on the beach in the late afternoon, frolicked in the water, teased each other about the hippie look-the long hair and the mod clothes they had grown accustomed to wearing. There was talk about love-ins, rock festivals, and the drug scene. With a battery operated radio they danced to the Beatles' *She Loves You*, drank Cokes and munched on chicken and chips, and laughingly reflected on their lives growing up in America. It was another happy gathering of beautiful young men and women who had volunteered to be a part of an operation called Sigma.

Later they assembled in small groups preparing for the interview scheduled for eight o'clock that night with Alexandria Day who lived on the island. "I don't know about the others," Julius Andrews said, "but I'm going to be a rancher."

"Too isolated a life for me," Curtis O'Connor said. "I'd rather live in a big city, but I have no idea what I'll be doing. I'll leave that up to Alexandria."

"What if she tells you to enter medical school and become a doctor?" Julius asked with a smile.

"Then that would be her decision, but you know as well as I do that she wouldn't choose a medical career for any of us, not if the original plan is to be followed."

Lisa overheard him, leaned back on her elbows, and said, "Curtis, do you really think we can accomplish all that Alexandria has in mind?"

He nodded. "With a little help from the others around the country. I've heard our people are everywhere, in just about every walk of life. They're looking to the twelve of us as the future strategic policy team, to be in position shortly after the turn of the century. We've got our work cut out for us, and I'm excited about the role I'm going to play, whatever that may be."

"Hey," Merriam hollered, "Carlton has an idea. We know in a few years we're going to be working together as a team, so he thinks we should name ourselves the Club of Apollo. What do you think?"

Jason Miller said, "Ah, Apollo, the god of light, foreteller of the future, the great musician and poet. Quite a mysterious fellow."

"Maybe we could have decoder rings," Fredcrick Craig said, "a password to get into our hiding place, a secret handshake."

After the laughter died down, Frank Jessops said, "I like the idea. In some ways we are a club, and nothing can keep us apart." He paused for a moment.

"Have any of you given any consideration as to what might happen if our true identities are discovered?"

"Yes," Burton Obrey said, "another Valentine's Day massacre." He saw Lisa's expression quickly change. "But I don't think we should concern ourselves with the possibility of exposure. We've followed the plan to the letter and there's no reason--"

"You're right," Claudia said. "We came here to do a job under the deepest cover imaginable. Our mission will be accomplished." She looked around at the others. "Agreed?"

They all touched hands and spoke as one. "Agreed."

***

That night in Alexandria Day's office, a military career was selected for Frederick Craig and Frank Jessops, with West Point and the Naval Academy as the appropriate avenues for officer training. Merriam Livingston, Robert Ames, and Simon Ellenberg were to study law. For Carlton Matthews, teaching on the college level was to be the entry position for a subsequent move into government service. At his insistence, Julius Andrews could become a rancher, enter politics later. Burton Obrey, Lisa Jackson, Claudia Andrade, Curtis O'Conner, and Jason Miller would have a liberal arts education and become politically active immediately upon graduation.

The group would not see each other again in person until Merriam's marriage to George Vance three years later.

Chapter 4

Merriam Livingston-Vance paused from her remembrances and looked at the man sitting on a chair in the corner of the small room. "How do you feel?"

Carlton Matthews said, "Fine, but I am curious as to what the media is saying about our disappearances, and what the FBI is doing."

She grimaced. "Wild stories from every imaginable angle, but nothing close to the truth. And the FBI? Depends on which faction you're talking about."

He watched her slow pacing, smiled. "Merriam, I'm reminded of our get-together when we were eight, and seeing you doing what you're doing now. You walked up and down that beach after our little ceremony of pressing our hands in the sand. I had to go back to get you and bring you inside. Similar thoughts in your mind, then and now?"

She sat down in the other chair and leaned back, hands in her lap. "No, back then I was looking eagerly to the future." She shrugged. "Now, since it appears we won't be around much longer, my thoughts are turned to the past, the fun we all had when we met on the island, and how wonderful Charles and Anne were in helping me live what would be considered a normal life in this country. And finding George Vance in college. I didn't know he had been assigned to the group, and was delighted to see him again."

"And the wedding," Carlton said. "You were the first. It was quite a celebration with all of us there. We sang and danced most of the night, then followed you to the hotel for another round of toasts. Some contagious affair, that was. We all caught the marriage bug. I guess when George told us about the second wave that came in right after we did, we knew it wouldn't take long to find suitable partners."

"Marrying one of our own was the only proper course of action." She smiled. "And within a year the twelve had multiplied by two."

"Thank goodness. I know my life here has been much better having Eve at my side. Of course, with the twenty-four of us having such a close bond, it was almost as though we had our own little community. I guess family is a better word."

"It sure helped when we longed to be home," she said.

"Yes, but we adjusted to the American way of life early on by mixing and mingling with others as though we were one of them."

"Still it was our close association in later years that helped us meet our individual objectives," Merriam said. She thought for a moment. "I'm just glad I didn't have to run for political office. I don't think I would have found campaigning too pleasant."

Carlton laughed. "Me either. Do you remember when the polls said O'Conner would lose his senate race?"

"I sure do. That's when we put out the word to our people hidden in the rank and file to get active in his campaign. Good thing. He only won by a little more than three hundred votes."

"Merriam, it's been quite an adventure."

She looked up at the ceiling and sighed. "But we were not able to finish our assignment."

Carlton brought his chair over beside her and took her hand. "Merriam, you've made major changes in the structure of the United Nations, and I think I've played a significant role in the affairs of State. And look what the others have done. Ames has overhauled the Justice Department, Jessops and Craig have changed the entire warfare concept of the military, and Ellenberg. Look how he's influenced the Supreme Court. And the whole tone and pitch of Congress is different because of Obrey, Andrews, and the others."

"I'm amazed that no one got suspicious and began tracking our rise to power as a group."

"Perfect infiltration," Carlton said. "We were from different regions of the country with divergent backgrounds. As far as I know, there's only one outsider who might figure out who we are and the scope of our mission. I've left enough clues along the way." He saw the question in her eyes. "Because I felt he might be helpful to us at some point in time. I'm talking about my friend, Phillip Lansing."

She closed her eyes. "I don't see what he could do now. It's almost over."

He squeezed her hand. "Merriam, the mission *will* be successful. Others will follow in our steps, and they will complete what we came to do. And Phillip, with his print and broadcast media experience, can begin to reach and influence the general public in a way we couldn't."

"I know you're right. It's just that--"

She was interrupted by the sound of the door opening.

Chapter Five

"The police have dusted and vacuumed every room. No evidence of anything abnormal. I don't know what the director expects us to find. And anyway, the admiral was miles from here when he disappeared."

FBI Special Agent Rick Ellis, tall and angular, gray hair in a crew-cut, turned to his partner. "Maybe Mrs. Jessops wasn't. I don't know what we're looking for either, except possibly something irregular, something obvious."

"Obvious?" Agent Jay Koop asked.

"The Metro cops deal only with the obscure, what's hiding behind the glare. What stands out like your nose on your face is what they *don't* see."

Koop sighed, hands on his hips, a perplexed look on his face as he surveyed the large living room. "Yeah, and what I see is a man's well-lived in castle."

"Don't forget he's married."

"Okay, a couple's castle." Koop looked at the filled book cases and stacks of books and magazines on tables, a half burned log in the fireplace, prints of various sizes filling the wall space, the rugs new, furniture expensive. The classic fashionable environment one would expect for a joint chief.

The agent felt a sense of awe being in Admiral

Jessops' home. At the same time he was uneasy, as though the big black man with the booming voice would suddenly march through the door demanding an explanation for the intrusion. At five-eight, the agent imagined looking up at the six-four muscular frame of the navy's top fighting man. He didn't relish the thought.

The two agents went into the kitchen. No messages under magnets on the refrigerator, little inside except milk and juice and a head of lettuce, no clutter on the counters, only another small pile of books on a bench near the breakfast table. Ellis scanned the titles, said, "Have you noticed that there's not a book anywhere dealing with the subject of warfare?"

Koop shook his head. "No, didn't pay much attention."

"Nothing on the Civil War, or the first and second world wars, not even anything relating to historical conflicts, naval battles, warships, or warfare strategy and tactics. Strange for a military man."

Koop asked, "What does he read?"

Ellis pitched him a book. "Stuff like this one. *Man's Social Nature and Interpersonal Experiences*, reading material for a sociologist or psychologist. He's got a small library in the living room on cultural heritage and forms of collective behavior."

Koop put the book back on the bench and opened the pantry door. Looks like Mrs. Jessops' behavior pattern was to eat out a lot, hardly a basic staple in here. Reminds me of my place."

Ellis smiled. "I've been trying to tell you, Jay, you've got to get yourself married."

"The admiral is, and it hasn't done much for his larder." They laughed, and Koop said, "Let's go look at the bedrooms." The agents climbed the stairs, and after carefully observing the master bedroom and the two guest rooms, Koop remarked, "There are no pictures of the admiral or his wife anywhere, no family history. You'd think there would be a few personal photos on the wall."

"Sure would. She has the face and figure my wife would die for, and his super-hero looks would light up the silver screen. They're beautiful people, but I guess they didn't have to remind themselves of that." He opened the doors to the large closets. "Full. If they packed anything before they left they are sure traveling light. Notice the shoe racks. Empty spaces in each one for the shoes they were wearing."

Koop opened the jewelry box on the dresser. "Look at this. Diamond earrings, emerald bracelet, a variety of rings with expensive stones, pearls and gold necklaces. Good stuff. Rick, I'm getting the impression that their departure was very sudden and dramatic. Got to be a kidnapping. Maybe terrorists got to the admiral at Andrews, drugged him and put him in the trunk of a car. With the right credentials, getting on and off the base would be a simple matter. Then they came back here and abducted Mrs. Jessops."

"The reports from Naval Intelligence could possibly support that theory even though they've discounted it," Ellis said. "The admiral was talking to his aides in the VIP lounge when he was called to the telephone in the base commander's office. When the plane was ready for boarding they went over to get him. He wasn't there. No one had seen him."

"And no one saw him go back through the gate. That's what makes it seem like an abduction to me."

Ellis opened another door, this one leading from the bedroom to the admiral's study. Again no photographs, military books or naval paraphernalia.

"Maybe there's something in his personal papers," Ellis said. He opened the top drawer of the desk. A ballpoint pen, two pencils, paper clips and a blank yellow pad. The side drawers produced only nature magazines, a pocket diary with nothing written in it, and file folders with real estate papers, titles to automobiles, and tax returns. "Not a bill, checkbook, or the normal paper-junk that litters most home work-stations."

"Doesn't make sense," Koop said.

"None of it does. Come on, let's get out of here."

***

Later that afternoon at FBI headquarters, six pairs of Federal agents compared their notes in preparation for a summary report for the director. The Ellis and Koop observations were essentially duplicated by the other teams. Except for closets full of clothes and some jewelry, few personal effects were found in the homes, each dwelling giving the appearance of a part-time residence. And though it could not be explained how

Admiral Jessops got past the guard at the air base, or how the others eluded friends and associates, the consensus was they had left on their own accord with no force or struggle involved.

Chapter 6

FBI Special Agent Norman Rigler parked on the narrow gravel road in the Virginia countryside, lights out. Night hung like a heavy black curtain blowing in the wind, an occasional flash of lightning momentarily framing the old tin-roofed farm house in the valley below. Rigler knew the house was deserted, property foreclosed. The perfect site for a bogus hit-and-run operation by agents of the task force. That's what Rigler's superior had asked for, a lure, a United States senator the supposed target. Only one other agent was called in for the assault.

Rigler lit a cigarette, took a drag and looked at his watch. Almost midnight. A moment later, car lights appeared in his rear view mirror. Agent James Craddock was on time. Rigler liked Craddock, his passion for intelligence work, how he often charted his own aggressive course in an investigation. Both in their early forties and single, they regularly jogged together, played macho studs in D.C.'s watering holes, and for a time dated twin sisters.

But in recent weeks Craddock had turned sour, wasn't the same man. Obviously angry, he expressed misgivings about the unit's mission, distanced himself from other agents. He was now considered a liability by the head of the task force.

The gray Ford pulled up behind. Rigler got out of his car, waved, and eased into the passenger seat beside his friend. "Hell of a night, and the temperature's dropping.

Craddock asked, "Where are the others?"

"I thought we could handle this ourselves."

"Are you sure Senator Obrey and his wife are in the house?"

Rigler removed his gloves. "My question earlier. I slipped down there and checked. Not a sign of life." He sighed. "The intel was faulty."

Craddock gripped the steering wheel, spoke softly. "As usual." He turned to look at Rigler. "Norman, why'd you pick me for tonight? You know how I feel about this stupid crusade. It's--"

"Jimmy, relax. I called because I wanted you personally involved, to get you back in sync with the mission. The twelve we're after are *evil*--against everything we believe in--and if our country is to survive, they've got to be terminated."

"*Jesus!* These are top government officials, elected and appointed, and there's not an ounce of proof they're not who they say they are. I can't believe you bought into this ridiculous fantasy." He shook his head. "I want out."

Rigler put his hand on Craddock's shoulder. "Jimmy, we took an oath, signed on to be a part of Task Force Zero until the entire group was eliminated." He paused. "We knew the consequences if we backed out."

Craddock forced a laugh. "Come on, Norman, this

is *America*. We work for the Federal Bureau of Investigation, not a terrorist militia in some downtrodden country. Consequences? I can't see agents popping agents because of the insanity of one man."

Rigler pulled away, lit a cigarette. "Why did you agree to be a part of the team?"

Craddock lowered the window, fanned the smoke away. "I got caught up in the excitement of a possible *real* conspiracy like the one in *Seven Days in May*, but this time it wasn't the military supposedly attempting a coup. We were dealing, so I thought, with traitors in the inner circle, and like you, I was gung ho to protect my country. Later I realized this was a crazy out-of-the-loop operation orchestrated by a mother-dominated fanatic. That's when I confided in you, thinking we could get out together and squash this thing." He shifted in his seat. "Have you told anyone about our conversation?"

Rigler lied. "No, no one. How about you? Any talk outside our group?"

Craddock hesitated. "Not yet."

"Okay, it's just between us. And to be honest, the reason I asked you to meet me tonight was to talk some sense into you." He glanced out the window. "But I guess you're not going to change your mind."

Craddock rubbed a hand over his face. "This was all a set-up, wasn't it? Make me see things differently or take me out. Thank God we're friends."

Rigler removed the weapon from his shoulder holster. "You're right on all counts. I'm sorry, but orders are orders."

Craddock watched the squeeze of the trigger. The bullet pierced his head above the right eye, tore through bone and brain and out the open window.

The agent returned to his car, flashed the headlights three times. A black SUV with the clean-up crew moved up the hill from the farm house below.

Chapter 7

At WTCX-TV Channel Eleven in the nation's capital, Keri, given name Kerianne Winslow, stared somberly into the camera as the floor manager said, "Clear, good show."

In a late bulletin at the close of the six p.m. news, she had reported on a four car accident on Highway 1 that left two people dead. With the cut to the commercial, her expression remained serious. Turning to her co-anchor, Chance Patton, she said, "If you've got a few minutes, I'll buy you a drink across the street."

He smiled. "What's the occasion?"

She removed the clip-on mike from her navy single-button suit, her voice low. "I got a tip before we went on the air that might add something to the missing VIP scuttlebutt."

The smile faded. "That's all it is, Keri, pure speculation, nothing verified. I'd rather not play the rumor game."

"I may have something new, only a drink's worth though. I'll meet you outside." They went to their respective offices to pick up coats. Chance was waiting for her at the side door, and held her arm down the sidewalk and across the slushy street.

Keri was tall and slender with shoulder length

honey-blond hair and dark blue eyes. Stocky, preppie Chance with contrasting dark hair and eyes, was a pretty boy with a well-modulated radio voice. Keri had heard his real name was Cecil but never asked him about it. She was in her early thirties, Chance ten years older. They had worked well as the early evening anchor team for the past year. Neither were married. The brief conversation from station to bar was on the early snow and Mark Games' "it's only going to get worse" weather report.

Finding two stools by the door in the sparsely crowded bar, they ordered a draft beer. "And fill up the peanut bowl," Keri said as she slipped out of her all-weather coat and folded it on her lap. Chance kept his on. "Now what's this about a hot tip?"

She leaned close. "The first we heard about the disappearances was in the newsroom a few days ago when something came in on the wire about Merriam Livingston-Vance, our UN Ambassador. Right?"

Chance rolled his eyes. "Another example of someone getting carried away, pardon the pun. The report said she was missing and the authorities had been called in. Then later a correction came through, said she and her husband had quietly left town for a well-earned rest in New Hampshire, that the wire service should have checked it out before stirring things up."

The drinks delivered, Keri popped a peanut in her mouth. "Yeah, but it makes you wonder why there was such an initial hullabaloo for something that could be explained away so easily." She held up her beer. "Here's to finding out why."

They clinked their glasses and took a sip, Chance adding, "And to professional reporting."

Keri continued. "And yesterday we hear a couple of the guys talking about Senator Obrey and Justice Ellenberg. Seems someone got a tip that the cops were looking for them. Foul play was suspected because they weren't where they were supposed to be. But a follow-up produced nothing; they weren't lost after all. Then this morning the buzz was that Secretary Matthews' limo was found with the motor running, doors locked, no one inside. Weird. And during make-up before we went on the air, I received a phone call."

He nodded. "Finally we're getting to the ever-thickening plot. Another missing person?"

She retrieved another peanut and chewed it. "It was a man, wouldn't give his name. He said that for some reason, which is our job to determine, our esteemed decision-makers are on the run with carefully planned no-trace escapes from the city. He said as of mid-afternoon today, a dozen top people left suddenly, including members of Congress and the Court, Cabinet officers, and key military personnel.

"When I started to quiz him, he hung up." She paused when she saw a bright flash of light in the mirror behind the bar, realized it was a reflection of headlights from a passing car. She smiled inwardly. A new light. That's what was needed in solving this mystery, a different approach to finding the truth. She would think about it later.

Chance touched her arm. "And?"

She glanced in the mirror again, gathered her thoughts. "Then I phoned the president's press secretary for confirmation, and he laughed at me. Harley said it was nothing but previously scheduled out-of-city meetings, yearly physical exams, and vacations. Roland at AP said he'd heard the reports but hadn't been able to get any corroboration. He's still digging, and so will I, until I have something to take to the boss."

Chance set his glass down gently on the coaster. "You know, Keri, I really can't get excited about his. They were probably just given time off for good behavior."

She brushed aside his attempt at humor and brought up the caller again. "I thought the voice sounded familiar, but I can't put a face or name to it yet. Maybe I'll call everyone in my book for a voice check. Anyway, I know someone from one of the networks assigned to the White House. He may be able to shed some light on this. He's in New York for a couple of days for a meeting of network correspondents. I'm having dinner with him tomorrow night."

"Are you talking about Phillip Lansing?" Seeing her nod, he let out a sigh. "Lansing won't know anything substantial before we do. Why don't you just leave it alone. This isn't the first time the big dealers have skipped out for some R and R. I think you're overreacting."

Keri straightened up, her voice cold. "Whoever made that phone call wasn't someone playing games. He knew more than he said, and the very fact that he called *me* means something. No, I'm going to stay on this until I have something to go with."

Chance motioned for the bartender, a totally bald heavy-set black man with an eyebrow ring and *love is the answer* tattooed on his right arm. "Avery, have you heard about anything unusual going on in town?"

Avery picked up a towel and wiped the counter. "Sure, and I wondered why you people didn't say anything about it on the six o'clock news."

"We're known for responsible journalism," Chance said, "nothing but the facts."

"Avery, what do you know?" Keri asked.

He glanced at the other patrons and spoke softly. "From the Supreme Court building to the Washington Monument, security is tighter than on inauguration day. But what I hear, most people won't notice it. No uniformed cops."

Keri asked casually, "What do you think is the reason for the concern?"

The bartender threw the towel over his shoulder. "The word is some top bureaucrats and military people are being abducted by terrorists of the domestic variety."

Chance shook his head. "Yeah, with a whole lot of other people just standing around watching."

Keri kicked his foot. "Where did you hear this?"

"My wife waits tables at the Jockey Club over at the Ritz-Carlton. She overheard it at lunch today when she was pouring coffee for a couple of bigwigs. Then at another table she heard someone say that dozens of officials are missing. Some are probably hiding. But you know what I think?"

"I can't wait to hear," Chance said.

Avery ignored the sarcasm. "The way I see it is some radicals got hold of that antimatter device the government's been keeping under wraps for years, and they vaporized our people."

Chance roared with laughter. "Oh my God, you can't be serious!"

"Sure am. That thing reverse the electrical charges in matter and annihilates it, turns matter into energy, the kind found in gamma rays. It literally dissolves people on the spot without even a puddle on the floor. Kind of spooky, if you ask me. Wonder who'll be next?"

Chance had his head on his arm, still shaking with laughter. "Avery, we've never had such a thing. Where did you get this nonsense?"

"Read about it a few months ago in one of the tabloids. They called it the ultimate weapon. Makes sense to me."

"Thanks, Avery," Keri said. She downed her beer. "Chance, I've got to go. More snow on the way, which is a perfect excuse for a quiet evening at home curled up with a good book. "She paid the bill and Chance helped her with her coat.

She turned back to Avery. "Tell your wife to keep listening. We won't mention names, but any scrap of information could mean something."

The big man smiled. "I got you."

Walking across the street to the parking garage,

Chance said, "Thanks for the beer, and if my advice means anything, I'd go easy on the probes. You might be getting in over your pretty head and--"

"What are you saying?"

"That you just might uncover something that puts you in danger. I wouldn't like that. "

She stared at him for a moment, then turned and walked briskly to her car without speaking, puzzled about what Chance might know and wasn't telling her. He wasn't the cautious type, particularly concerning a story. She'd pin him down tomorrow and get it out of him.

***

As Keri opened the door to her apartment the phone was ringing. She immediately recognized the voice as the man who had called her earlier at the station. "Ms. Winslow, are the twenty-four dead or alive?"

She took a deep breath. "So now the number has doubled."

"Count the spouses, Ms. Winslow. They're missing, too."

Keri ran a hand through her hair. "Look, I don't know what their condition is or why you're calling me. I'm in the dark about this like everyone else."

"You have sources. *Dig*, lady, *dig*. Don't just accept what's coming in on the wire or what you hear from other journalists. Use your imagination, call in some favors, and find out who or what is behind this."

"Why don't you, whoever you are."

There was a long silence. Finally the voice said, "I can't, but you can. Now listen. Underwood's approval rating is higher than for any president since polling for such nonsense began, and for the most part the country has pulled together in a way seldom experienced in peace time. But you know what will happen if the word gets out that our top people are running. There will be a panic and this administration will be destroyed."

Keri unbuttoned her coat and sat down in the blue velvet wing chair. "I'm sorry, but there's nothing I can do about that. If you know me, you also know I'm second tier anchor at a local TV affiliate, not a network sleuth or a Bernstein-Woodward who's about to be tapped on the shoulder by an all-knowing insider."

The man on the line sighed. "You used to be a damned good investigative reporter, but I guess you've lost your fire. Sorry I bothered you."

With the disconnect, Keri replaced the receiver and leaned back in the chair to think. He's got to be someone in the president's inner circle. There was both fear and anger in his voice. She replayed his words in her mind and began to sense something more than just the protection of Samual Underwood's popularity. He was fearful about what might happen to this country. What if the president and vice president disappeared, too? Lord, this government could be in real trouble. Suddenly she felt a chill of her own apprehension. She wanted to talk to Phillip.

Phillip Lansing, mid-forties, tall and lean with a craggy face and brown hair and eyes, was different than most men Keri had dated. He was sensitive and strong, intellectual but with an earthy quality. She knew she was falling in love with him and could tell he felt something for her, but his divorce a year ago had set him free from what he called a terribly possessive woman. She guessed he wasn't ready for a permanent relationship. That would change if Keri had her way.

She checked her answering machine to see if he had called. Nothing but hangups. Phillip would have left a message. She wished she knew where he was staying in New York.

Thinking of Phillip had settled her nerves. She smiled. Maybe the two of them could get to the bottom of this disappearance act. With that thought, she took off her coat and went into the kitchen to fix something to eat, her mind flipping through names that could possibly shed some light on the mysterious vanishings. Only Phillip Lansing stayed with her through the evening.

Chapter 8

Wallace Brent felt his wife pressing against his back as she pulled up the blanket, the warmth of body and breath dispelling the chill he had felt from tossing the covers in his sleep. It had been a fitful night. He looked at the red numbers on the digital clock: 4:03. The automatic timer on the coffee pot was set for four-fifteen, the alarm for fifteen minutes later. He was wide awake now, but would let Millie snuggle and doze until the music came on and the coffee aroma wafted into the bedroom.

He thought about the day ahead and hoped it would be more productive than the previous one. Another early morning meeting with the president had been scheduled; a top echelon conference at FBI headquarters later in the day.

Millie rubbed his shoulder. "You're tensing," she whispered, "I can feel it."

He turned over and took her in his arms. "What would we do today if I was retired?"

"Oh, I don't know," she said softly, "maybe take off for the Bahamas, sip exotic drinks and build sandcastles, take a sailboat ride at sunset."

"I'd rather fly to London, shop for some new tweeds, stay at the Connaught and dress formerly for dinner. We could take in a play and--"

"My *de bon aire* husband." She pulled him closer. "To be honest, darling, just being at home with you and with the telephone unplugged would be fine with me."

Millicent Brent was in her late fifties with dark brown hair and eyes and a trim figure maintained in a daily aerobics class. She and Wallace had been married more than thirty years. Their son Jeffrey, with his chiseled features and large frame in the image of his father, worked for an oil company in Houston. His semi-annual visits were too infrequent for her. "Or we could go see Jeff and Sharon. The baby's nearly a year old now and we could start learning how to play grandparents."

He raised his head and looked at her with a grin. "On second thought, I don't think I'm ready to retire, particularly if it involves baby sitting. I'll wait until young Wally grows a bit and stops squalling. Might even teach him how to fish."

Millie leaned up and kissed him on the nose. "You've never fished in your life."

"I like the picture. Old man and boy sitting in a boat with poles in hand and talking philosophically about life. It would feel good."

She gave him a loving smile. "So would a vacation, and London's fine with me. It's been so long since we spent any time outside the Beltway. Slipping away for a few days would be good for both of us."

He let her go and swung his legs to the floor, the reverie broken, reality returning. "That's what too many people have been doing lately, slipping away." He rubbed his eyes. "And I can't keep a lid on it much longer. The whole thing is going to break open soon, and it's going to be panicsville on the Potomac. And we still haven't found Craddock, Walsh and Patino."

"You're missing agents."

He nodded. "I don't know what to think, Federal agents don't just disappear."

She touched his arm. "You want to talk about it?"

"Nothing else to say. Stay here. I'll go turn up the heat and get us a cup of coffee. Should be ready by now."

He was in the kitchen when the telephone rang. Millie sunk back on the pillow. She wished she and Wallace could disappear, too.

***

FBI Agent Norman Rigler picked up the car telephone, dialed a residence in Bethesda. The voice on the other end of the line sounded half awake. "Yeah, what is it?"

"This is Rigler. I'm parked on the street near Senator Obrey's house. I believe he and his wife are in there."

The agent in Bethesda was more alert now. "What makes you think so?"

"His car's in the driveway, and I saw a light upstairs. It was on and off pretty fast, might have been a flashlight. Appears they came back looking for something and don't want to attract any attention. Do you want me to follow the original plan?"

"Absolutely. I think I remember a hedge on the side of the driveway."

"I see it," Rigler said.

"Get out of your car and wait for them there. When they leave the house, pop them. And I'm assuming you've chosen the proper weapon."

"Yes sir, untraceable, ballistics meaningless, and I'm using a silencer."

"I'll be waiting for your report."

Agent Rigler slipped quietly out of the car, gun in hand. He was almost to the driveway when he heard two car doors closing. He crouched down behind the hedge, and when the engine started he rose and fired twice through the driver's side window. The street lamp provided sufficient light to see the driver slump over on the steering wheel. He then turned his gun to the passenger trying frantically to open the door on the other side, ample time for the agent to aim and spit lead through glass.

Rigler looked around at the neighboring homes. No lights. All quiet. His boss would be pleased.

Chapter 9

*Falling, falling, plunging into a grave so quiet...
dead, covered with green in the darkness deep. Sorry,
Keri, you knew too much.*

Keri sat up in bed, eyes wide open, perspiration on
her forehead, a sense of foreboding knifing through her
as the voice continued to echo in her mind. *Oh, God,
what was that about?* She got up and went to the
bathroom and washed her face in cold water, then sat
down on the edge of the bathtub, head in hands. Her
own fears projected in a dream? Had to be. She stood
and took deep breaths to settle her nerves.

She returned to the bedroom and looked at the
clock. Almost six. She switched on the television for the
morning news, paused as a UN official reported on the
overthrow of communism in North Korea and the
planned merging of the Koreas. She changed channels.
More pharmaceutical companies declaring bankruptcy.
Still nothing on the missing people. She went to the
kitchen to make coffee.

She thought again about the caller....*you've lost
your fire*. Was she burned out? Maybe that's what
frightened her. She saw her reflection in the kitchen
window. At first glance it was the face of a young girl.
Innocent. Too pretty for TV news said her professor in
college, an equation with no smarts and a lack of power
in her demeanor. That made her more determined than

ever to be a TV newswoman. The drive was there, the ambition to succeed at whatever she did, and it had stayed with her through the years.

She learned the art of head and shoulder language, and practiced working with her eyes in tandem with a stronger delivery to be both authoritative and reassuring. Keri also let her intelligence and wit shine through to reflect a more well-informed, mature image. Later on the job, in Baltimore and in Washington, she had volunteered for field reporting assignments other TV news people looked upon as beneath them.

She developed her extemporary skills and became a highly professional reporter admired by her peers, yet she seemed to be stuck, along with Chance Patton on the early evening news. Erickson had said the late night anchors had the ratings. "You don't fix something that isn't broken." Interesting, she thought. Both were past middle-age and grim. Good for them. That's what the people obviously wanted.

She reached into the frig and removed the orange juice container and filled a glass. But what did she want now? She knew. A lasting relationship with Phillip.

The ringing phone jarred her. It was Erickson. "Keri, we just heard two people were shot to death outside Senator Obrey's home. The cops think it may be the senator and his wife. I've got a van heading over there and I want you to cover the story."

"He's on the missing list. Do you think the others--"

"One situation at a time, Keri."

"I'm not dressed yet, Randall. Call Tonya or Chance. I'm supposed to cover the genetics symposium this morning."

"I'll send someone else over there, and you know our other anchors don't like to get their hands dirty with on-site reporting. No, it's your assignment, so throw on your coat and get hopping." He gave her directions to the site of the murders.

"I'll be there in twenty minutes."

She gulped the juice and ran to the bedroom closet, where she slipped on a wool knit dress and boots. Keri's natural beauty was a definite plus for unplanned on-camera appearances. Little had to be done except a quick brush through her golden hair and a touch of lipstick and blush. Ten minutes later she was out the door with coat in one hand and a cup of coffee in the other. Burned out? Hardly.

***

Keri pulled in behind the WTCX van, saw Tim Holt leaning against the yellow ribbon stretched across the street, camera on shoulder, videotaping the scene for later background footage. The normally quiet residential street of palatial homes had been transformed into a frenzy of flashing lights, tight lipped cops, vocally obnoxious media types and curious spectators. She moved beside him and asked, "What have you heard?"

Holt pointed to a man in hat and topcoat standing in the secured area near a car. He was shouting instructions to uniformed officers. "That's Detective Smith. He's in charge. All I've got so far is that the bullet-ridden car belongs to Senator Obrey, but no one has said if there are any bodies in there or not."

"I know Smith, follow me." Keri ducked under the ribbon with Holt behind her. As a cop held up his hand to halt the pair, she hollered at the detective. "Lloyd!" He turned in her direction.

Smiling, she said, "Forgive the informality, Detective Smith. You remember me, I'm Keri Winslow, Channel Eleven."

"Let them through," Smith said, "but hold the others back for now."

Keri whispered to Holt as they walked. "I praised him on-air for solving the murder at the Botanic Garden, said Metro needed more professionals like him. A week later he was promoted and sent me a thank-you note. Roll the tape as soon as I'm in position. Get it all and we'll edit later."

Keri shook the detective's hand warmly, then stepped back for a head and shoulders two-shot. She let the tape roll for a few seconds to allow the studio lead-in. "I'm here with Detective Lloyd Smith of Washington MPD. Detective, is it true that Senator Obrey and his wife have been murdered?"

Smith pushed his hat back to offer a fuller view of his round face. "The vehicle is registered to Senator Burton Obrey, and while we haven't yet found either the senator or his wife, it appears they may have been victims of a shooting."

Keri said, "What do you mean, *may* have been? Please tell us what happened here."

The detective rubbed his chin. "The driver's side window was pierced by multiple gunshots. And from the blood patterns on both sides of the car, on the seats, steering wheel and passenger side dash and floor, it's obvious two people were in there. And the bodies were removed. There's blood on the snow on both sides of the car."

Keri asked, "At approximately what time did the shootings occur?"

"About quarter to five this morning. No one heard shots. The assailant may have used a silencer. A neighbor was up and heard an engine start and looked out his window to see a car accelerating down the street with its lights off. Then he saw the senator's car with both front doors standing open. That's when he got suspicious."

"The neighbor called the police."

The detective nodded. "That's right."

"Do you have a description of the car?"

"Only that it was black."

"But you're not sure who was in the senator's car. It could have been someone else."

"Possible, but I doubt it. It *was* their car, and the attack took place at the end of the driveway to their home. That's all I can tell you now." He pulled his hat down and walked back to talk to a man in a trench coat taking pictures of the car.

Keri turned to the camera. "This is Keri Winslow, Channel Eleven, Eyewitness News." As Holt removed the cassette from the camera and ran toward the van,

Keri spotted Ken Sigler of the *Post*. He was talking to a man she recognized as Tony Voger, head of the FBI's domestic intelligence operation. Seeing the two men shake hands and turn away, she approached Sigler.

"Good morning, Keri. I'm assuming you didn't get much either, just a blood-stained car with no bodies. More intrigue adding to the mystery."

Keri shook her head. "Dead or alive, people are still missing. I wish I knew what was going on."

"Yeah, me too. I was just asking Agent Voger about the possible burglaries."

"You're ahead of me. What are you talking about?"

"One of the guys at the paper is a close friend of Senator O'Connor's aide, Marvin King. King told him there have been break-ins at the homes and offices of two of the missing twelve, O'Connor and Speaker Andrews."

"Any details?" Keri asked.

"Voger said it never happened, but I'm not so sure. King had first hand information. He told the cops he came back to O'Connor's office about midnight to pick up some papers, and as he rounded a corner in the hall he caught a glimpse of a man taking the stairwell exit. When King went in the office and noticed a cabinet drawer partially opened, one that contained the senator's private papers, he immediately ran down to the parking garage. He got there in time to see a gray sedan leaving."

"Did he get a license number?"

"Yeah. The car belongs to Cliff Manor, an FBI agent. Metro police are trying to track him down for questioning, but Voger said Manor has been out of town on assignment for the past week, said O'Connor's aide misread the numbers. I don't know. There's just too many odd pieces; nothing fits in the puzzle."

Keri asked, "Did the aide report anything missing from the office?"

"Everything seemed to be accounted for."

They moved out of the way to allow the police wrecker to back in. Keri said, "They'll haul the car downtown and check for matching blood types. At least we'll know something then."

Sigler smiled. "We ran a little filler piece on Senator Obrey and his wife, Helen, about a year ago when we heard they didn't have a doctor and refused to have physical exams. They didn't give us much of a story except to say they were blessed with good health, which they attributed to staying away from doctors and hospitals. I'll bet there's no record of their blood types."

Keri rolled her eyes. "Oh great. No confirmation. This is getting ridiculous."

"Yes. And to use an old expression, I've got a feeling we ain't seen nothin' yet."

***

Keri called Erickson at the station on her cell phone, saying Holt was on his way with the tape and reported on what Sigler had told her. She said she would try to talk to someone on the senator's staff later in the morning, and then do a follow-up with Detective Smith.

"But first I'm going back to my apartment, have a bite to eat and fix up a bit. Call me there if you need me."

"We'll cut out a segment on the noon news for you if you get anything solid on the senator or the burglaries. Call it in and we'll record it for playback. And Keri, call Harley over at the White House and see if the president has anything to say about the senator."

"Randall, we don't know who was in that car." She hesitated. "I'll check with the press secretary."

"We'll be waiting for your call."

***

There was a message from Phillip on Keri's answering machine. He would arrive early evening from New York and would meet her at Vincenzo's restaurant at eight o'clock.

She reheated the coffee and had a breakfast of fruit and toast, then called Mark Harley at the White House. His secretary said he was out and didn't know when he would return.

Next she punched in Senator Obrey's office and asked for Linda Posey, his executive assistant. Keri held for over two minutes. When Posey came on the line, she apologized for the delay, said no statement would be forthcoming until definite word had been received from the police.

She sounded so nonchalant, not a trace of concern in her voice. Keri poured another cup of coffee and decided to wait until later in the morning to contact Detective Smith. She would do so in person.

Chapter 10

It was like a Sunday morning. Streets practically deserted, and Director Brent knew why. He could tell concern was growing when he saw small groups of residents gathered in their front yards as he drove through Georgetown. As though a serial killer was loose in the neighborhoods, shops normally open by this time were still dark.

The rumors were rampant, and fear was being laid on top of fear, weighing everyone down, which dread unknowns will do. And the whisperings at the Bureau showed him no one was immune. He wondered if the president knew more than he was saying.

***

President Underwood was standing in the middle of the Oval Office staring at the floor when the director entered. Unshaven, hair tousled, a cup of coffee in his hand, he appeared deep in thought. He looked at Brent and his eyes came alive. "Hello, Wallace. I guess you've heard about what happened at Senator Obrey's home. I know he wasn't in the car, but two people were obviously killed. Do you have any further information?"

"I got a call on the car phone on the way over here. Metro police are at the scene, and Mr. President, they believe that Senator and Mrs. Obrey were the victims. I know they were good friends of yours. I'm sorry."

"I don't think they were in the car. Let's move on

to something else."   Realizing the president was cutting off further discussion of the murders, Brent said, "Sir, Assistant Director Gillespie called me at home early this morning. We now have information on the adoption situation that may interest you."

The president walked over and leaned against his desk. "I'm listening."

"I know this may sound strange, but it appears all twelve of the missing people were adopted."

The president put his cup down. "Are you sure?"

"Yes, sir. And while there is no record of any court proceedings, our preliminary information indicates that in each case the child came to live with a family at the age of seven. Former friends and neighbors we tracked down say they assumed the parents obtained the right to custody by an adoption decree, that the natural parents were said to be deceased. But they don't recall any background investigations, no contact by any agency for character references."

"Maybe each couple simply took the child into the family without securing a legal relationship, as in *loco parentis*, in the place of parents." He walked around his desk and sat down.

Settling in his usual spot on the sofa, the director said, "Could be." He looked at his notes. "Oh, yes. One of the neighbors remembered back when the new little boy came to live next door. She said he had a strange accent, not American, foreign. That boy grew up to be our attorney general, Robert Ames. When my agents specifically quizzed others about the manner of speech for each child, we got the same thing. Most common reference was European."

The president nodded.

"Something else peculiar. When the children entered college, after graduating at the top of their class I might add, the parents left town and were not heard from again. Same pattern for all twelve, and we haven't been able to find any of them."

"Most unusual," the president said.

"Yes it is." He hesitated. "Sir, have you heard of *Ordensburgen?*"

"German."

"Yes, sir. It means Order Castles, schools in Germany at the beginning of the second World War to train Nazi elite along the lines of the Teutonic Knights of the fourteenth century. It was believed several top SS officers escaped to Switzerland as the war was coming to an end. There was later speculation that in the fifties they found the brightest *Kinder-Ordensburgen*, children of the order still living in Germany, and arranged to have them sent to loyal parents in America to be the new Reich leaders in a future age."

The president smiled. "You don't think--"

"Sir, my job is to consider every possibility."

His face hardened. "You're implying the twelve who disappeared are traitors, undercover agents of a power rising in the shadows, part of a modern day fifth column. I can't buy that. I know these people personally, and I'd stake my life on their integrity and love of this country."

"Be careful about climbing out on limbs, Mr. President. People are not always who they seem to be."

"Wallace-" He paused to answer the telephone.

As the president listened to the voice on the other end, he slowly turned in the swivel chair away from Brent, who could see only the top of his head, his words unintelligible. Moments later he swung around. "Wallace, top government people in countries all over the world, including Germany, are now missing. This is no longer a domestic situation, it's global. And you can forget about a new breed of Teutonic Knights."

***

Unlike the preened and suited correspondents who had attended the network meeting in New York earlier that morning, Phillip Lansing was wearing a blue blazer, jeans, and a blue button-down shirt with no tie. He poured himself another cup of coffee, took a sip and frowned. Bad coffee. He moved to the window.

From the forty-eighth floor of the CBC building on Park Avenue, he had a bird's eye view of the masses below. Tiny people with their phobias and assorted bugaboos, all straining to find some measure of gratification, some understanding of the cards they'd been dealt. Now the deep concern about what was going on with their governing body contributing to the overload. He numbered himself among the anxious ones, especially after the meeting presided over by the network chairman, Jason Duke. Lansing couldn't believe the ridiculous mind-set, the denials of Duke and the top brass. No sweat, said Clyde Morgan, his boss.

Nothing to be concerned about, all part of a secret mission orchestrated by the White House.

He turned to look at Morgan leaning back in his swivel chair, hands locked behind his head. "You know what we've been told is a bunch of crap. Underwood doesn't operate this way. The guy's a nut about briefing the press in advance of any shifts in policy or international posturing, and he's taken some flack from Congress about being too open."

The news chief grinned, his ultra-white teeth a sharp contrast to his deeply tanned face and bald head. "Phillip, just because he's held more press conferences than any president in history doesn't mean we're privy to all that's going on. Some things are not told ahead of time. A government can't work that way on a consistent basis."

Phillip walked over and sat down in one of the wide leather chairs facing the desk. "Our illustrious chairman's little speech only stimulated more curiosity among the news team. And that secret mission bit is pure garbage. You know it, Morgan, and so do I."

"Not for me to know. That's the party line, and we're sticking to it from top to bottom. And that includes you."

Phillip leaned toward him, anger in his voice. "Well, then you'd better tell everyone to get on your phony train with their stories straight. Ambassador Livingston-Vance and her husband are said to be vacationing in New Hampshire. An aide said Speaker Andrews was on his ranch in Montana. General Craig is

supposedly at NATO headquarters in Brussels, and Justice
Ellenberg's senior clerk reported he was at some unspecified clinic in Arizona. All a pack of lies. Now the networks and cable news are saying the twelve are holed up somewhere near Montreal on some covert mission. More lies."

Morgan slid his chair back from the flashing eyes and lit a cigarette. "Sometimes there is safety in fabrication."

Phillip got up and walked back to the window, shaking his head. "Where did the fabrication originate."

"Near the top."

"*How* near the top?"

"I'd rather not say."

Probably Harley, the president's press secretary. "I'm going back to Washington this afternoon and blow a hole in this thing. Someone knows what's going on and--"

"You believe there's a conspiracy?"

Phillip leaned against the window and rubbed his jaw. "Only in conspiring to falsify information." He turned to face him. "Morgan, there's something you and the others around here may not know. Think for a moment who's missing. You've got a Supreme Court Justice, a UN Ambassador, two top military men, the Attorney General, the Secretary of State, the Speaker of the House, the Senate Majority Leader, and four other senators from both sides of the aisle. What do they all have in common?"

"They work for the government."

"Besides that, they're very close personal friends. Hardly a week goes by that they don't get together as a group, either in Washington or here in New York. With few exceptions they don't socialize with others. Hell, man, even when they go on vacations, two or more of the couples go together. Now what are the odds that this particular group would be sent off by the president to some secret meeting in Canada?"

Morgan squinted his eyes. "How do you know so much about them?"

"I watch what's going on and I listen. I know Carlton and Eve Matthews. He's a long-time friend, grew up in the same town together, and he's jokingly referred to the group as the Club of Apollo." He paused. "I think I'm the only outsider who knows this."

"In Greek mythology," Morgan said, "Apollo was the god of the sun. Was your friend implying something here?"

"Carlton said Apollo was also the archetype of truth, and it seems to me these people walk their talk in that area. They're known for their unquestioned integrity."

"So where has this honorable and distinguished coterie disappeared to? A spur of the moment cruise in the Grcck Isles?"

Phillip said, "My gut tells me they discovered something, either at the UN or in our government, something that put them in danger, perhaps life-threatening. Senator Obrey's car filled with bullet holes early this morning proves that. I figure they left town to regroup elsewhere and decide what to do, and I think I'll hear from Carlton. In the meantime, I want to do some snooping myself."

Morgan glanced down at the copy of a memo on his desk signed by Carl Cross, the president's national security advisor. "I'm afraid not, Phillip. You'll play the game with the rest of us."

"And if I don't?"

"The least of your troubles will be looking for another job."

***

Senator Claudia Ferguson put her arms around her husband Paul, asked in a soft voice, "Did you think it would end like this?"

He stroked her hair. "I've had a feeling for quite some time that we were being followed, especially during the past few weeks. So did Carlton. In fact, he believes we've been watched since we came to Washington. Remember when we went to Cozumel a few years back with Lisa and Ted?"

"Yeah, and the hurricane hit the hotel and they pad-locked us in the basement."

Paul led her to the small bench and they sat down. "I recognized Stanton Linitz in the crowd. I knew he was FBI and thought he might be on vacation. But he kept avoiding me. Every time I moved in his direction, he'd go the other way. Then he just suddenly disappeared."

"He probably got out into one of the underground

tunnels," Claudia said, "and waited until the storm had passed and got off the island."

"Maybe so. I think he was keeping an eye on us, and when he realized I had spotted him, he got nervous."

"You never mentioned this back then," Claudia said.

"I didn't want to make a big deal out of something I wasn't sure about. Anyway, from what we know now, it wouldn't have made any difference if I had confronted him. The wheels had already been set in motion from higher up."

"Then it was inevitable that we end up spending our final days here."

Paul looked at his beautiful wife, a slender dark haired woman with brown eyes. "I'm glad I found you when I did."

She took his hand. "It was the other way around. I found *you*. Remember I had gone to that fraternity party with Bud Wills, saw you standing with a group of guys at the bar. I waited until you turned around. Just like in the movies, our eyes met and that was it."

"There you were, the captivating Claudia Andrade, and I asked you to marry me less than a month later. Regrets?"

She smiled. "Not regarding our life together here; it's been perfect. I just wish the end of the movie had been scripted differently."

Chapter 11

Erickson called Keri shortly after ten o'clock. The two people murdered in Senator Obrey's car had been found, further information to be given at the police briefing at ten-thirty.

By the time Keri reached MPD headquarters at Third and C Streets, Captain Galvin was distributing sheets of paper to the assembled press. As she pushed through the crowd to get her copy, Galvin said, "It's all here, at least all we know at this time."

"Were Senator and Mrs. Obrey the murder victims?" Keri yelled.

The captain shook his head. "You're a little late on the take, lady. No, the Obreys were not in the car."

A bald heavy-set reporter from the *Post* said, "Give us a quick summary, your personal observations."

"A bungled burglary. Now for the rest of it, the victims have been ID'd as Gordon Muse and Joseph Napier, both with rap sheets of considerable length. They were found in the water earlier this morning near the Navy Yard, both shot through the head at close range. Glass particles from the bodies matches that of the driver's side window of Senator Obrey's automobile. Napier had a belt-pack on him containing what we believe are Mrs. Obrey's jewels. It appears the Obrey home was burglarized, and as the thieves were leaving in the Senator's car, a person or persons opened fire."

A man in back who Keri didn't recognize said, "It was dark when all this took place and the senator's car has tinted windows, so it would be difficult to see who was inside. Isn't it only logical to assume that Senator Obrey was the intended victim?"

The captain hesitated, said, "Only the shooter knows the answer to that question. We'll find him. Quote me on that."

A radio reporter raised her hand. Keri recognized her from other press briefings, hair in a crew-cut, masculine attire, deep voice. "Captain Galvin, I heard from one of your officers that another car was found in the vicinity of the senator's home. There's no mention of that in your report."

"It appears the perpetrators drove to the scene in a stolen vehicle, a fairly old model I might add, and decided to leave in the senator's new Town Car."

Keri held up her hand, asked, "Do you know where the senator and his wife are at this time?"

He frowned and stared at Keri for a couple of seconds before answering. "We've been told they are away for a few days and should return to the city by the weekend. Now that's all I've got. Any other questions should be answered in the release."

"One more question," Keri said. "What about the increased security in town?"

"No comment." The captain turned and left the room.

***

A call was made from a pay phone in Falls Church to extension forty-three in the J. Edgar Hoover Building in Washington, D.C. Hearing the pick-up, the caller asked, "Are you alone?"

"Yes."

"Sorry about the mix-up, but I've taken care of everything."

"Yeah, except Senator Obrey."

"I thought he and his wife were in the car. You'd have reached the same conclusion if you had been there."

"Maybe. At least you saved the tax-payers some money getting rid of those two hoods, but you should have left the bodies in the car. What were you thinking?"

"I didn't know who the men were. I thought at first they might be our people. I panicked. Then to clean up the scene, I put the bodies in the trunk."

"Did you dispose of the weapon?"

"Yeah, along with the mat from the trunk. As I said, everything's clean."

"All right, but stay away from Obrey's home until you can switch cars. Some neighbor saw a black vehicle leaving the scene."

"Damn."

"He couldn't identify the make and didn't get a license number, but Agent Manor wasn't so lucky. He was spotted leaving the building after breaking into Senator O'Connor's office. I sent him to Baltimore and set up internal paperwork to show he'd been there all week. We have to be more careful."

"What do you want me to do now?"

"Keep looking," the senior FBI agent said. "They're in the city somewhere. We've checked all the airlines, trains, and busses, and there's no record of any tickets purchased. Anyway, someone would have recognized them."

"Maybe they drove out of town."

"All private cars and service limousines are accounted for. Checks with the rental car agencies turned up nothing. Even though the official report is that they're in Canada, I know they're still in the area. And with all the attention the press is giving to them, I expect we'll have a tip soon."

"Have you considered the possibility that another group, maybe foreign, is responsible for their disappearances? We may not be the only ones tracking them."

"I thought about that and will continue to check it out through other intelligence sources, but it doesn't make sense to me. We would have picked up on another surveillance team. No, I still believe they're hiding."

"If that's the case, we'll get them."

The FBI man took a deep breath. "The sooner the better, and I want positive identification of each body. Pass that on."

He hung up and looked at the photograph of his mother on the credenza. "For you, Mom, for you."

Chapter 12

The late afternoon meeting in the FBI Director's office began with a discussion of the murders, with a decision to let Metro Homicide continue the investigation without Bureau interference. Next was an overview of the media frenzy focusing on the "wonder where" articles in the newspapers and the source-must-remain-anonymous reports on television. All added to the rumors of a possible takeover by the U.S. military, kidnapping by foreign volunteers allied with Saudi intelligence, and a mysterious virus that was descending upon the Capital.

A caller on a radio talk show insisted the Second Coming would occur on Saturday next. National Public Radio got into the act with a panel of psychologists discussing deep-seated national fears and the behavioral characteristics of those who feel they have been deserted by an authority figure, with therapy recommended as a way of overcoming depression, compulsions and anxieties. The program concluded with an appeal from the panel for the missing officials to return to their posts to alleviate the public pain suffered by their departure.

Director Brent shook his head. "At least it's just a guessing game for now and there's no mass hysteria, mainly because of the network reports. They're all denying the disappearances and saying the officials are attending a secret conference in Canada, details to be announced soon. The National Security Advisor worked that deal. Of course, it won't silence everyone, but we'll take all the help we can get."

Agent Benton Fowler, a tall, thin, mid-fifties man with a heavy crop of salt and pepper hair, said, "My mother called me last night from Nashville. If the rest of the country feels as she does, we've got a problem."

"Obviously she was upset," the director said.

"Mother doesn't like what she calls power vacuums, and she says her neighbors feel the same way. To hear her tell it, they are in a state of near panic. If this thing spreads, we may very well have that mass hysteria."

Brent breathed deeply. "Okay, Fowler, what else do you have?"

"From information found on the Internet, people calling themselves super patriots are saying our government is falling apart, that officials fearing a take-over are going into hiding, that the loyal sons of America must take advantage of this opportunity to strike."

Brent's jaw tightened. "Yeah, and the talk radio kooks are adding more fuel to the fire. One of our people in New York reported hearing a caller suggest the use of ricin to eliminate what he called the corrupt system and all those who are a part of it."

Fowler said, "And it's moved into other sectors.

One website for a religious group in Virginia particularly disturbed me. They say the Washington clowns are deserting the ship, so it's time to rip the underpinnings out from under the system and declare the Constitution null and void. They're promoting a theocracy."

"Keep an eye on them," Brent said, "and continue to monitor their activities."

Fowler smiled. "One of our people is on the inside."

"Good," Brent said. He looked at Tony Voger who headed up domestic intelligence operations. "What else?"

Voger was in his late forties, medium height and weight with sunken eyes and dark hair combed straight back. "All's quiet out there," Voger said, "not a single lead from any of the field offices to follow up on. But I do have agents looking deeper into the backgrounds of the missing twelve, going back to old teachers, preachers, et cetera. And we're also searching for any living parents."

Brent asked Assistant Director Kevin Gillespie to report on the adoption situation. "All of the children came to their new homes in nineteen fifty-four. Now that wouldn't be too odd, statistically speaking, if we were talking about country-wide adoptions. But we're looking at a small group of people who rose to key positions in the operation of this government, and that makes the pattern highly unusual."

Brent asked, "Any judgment on that?"

Gillespie shifted his round body in the chair. "Curiosity mostly. Why would twelve whiz kids suddenly appear with new families in one year? And where did they come from, and where did the adoptive parents disappear to when the children left for college? This is all very strange indeed."

"Any significance to nineteen fifty-four?" the director asked.

"Well, I knew it probably wouldn't have any bearing, but I checked it anyway, got a computer print-out of what was going on in this country at the time."

"I doubt if anything back then would tie into this case," Voger said.

"Unfortunately you're right, Tony. I had the analysts check the country's pulse on a day-to-day basis throughout that year, looking at media coverage of both major and minor events, and data in our files on investigative activities. There just wasn't anything that I could put my finger on relating to the children."

"Give us the major subject matter," Brent said.

Gillespie looked at his notes. "With Eisenhower's election in fifty-two, most people think of the fifties as a time of peace and prosperity, but there were a lot of simmering fears. We tested a hydrogen bomb in fifty-three. So did the Soviets. We followed up with another H-bomb explosion in fifty-four with Secretary of State Dulles calling for more retaliatory power. He said later that America would go to the brink of war if necessary. The Cold War was getting hotter and the country getting jittery. People even began to think about building backyard bomb shelters. I consider nineteen fifty-four as the beginning of a very critical period for this world."

Benton Fowler started to speak but Brent held up his hand to let Gillespie continue.

"Also in that year," Gillespie said, "the Atomic Energy Commission accused Oppenheimer, who played a principal role in the development of the atomic bomb, of being soft on communism and failing to be enthusiastic for the H-bomb. That's also the year of Senator McCarthy's Senate subcommittee hearings where he accused the Democrats of treason and hiding commies under every bed. The whole country not only had a case of nerves, but was becoming paranoid."

Brent nodded. "Anything else that stood out?"

"We're still looking."

"All right," Brent said, "let's take a different tack." He told the group about his conversation with the president concerning *Ordensburgen*, the possibility of sending children of the order to live with zealots in America in hopes of someday founding a new Reich. "I don't consider that proposition valid now, but the *idea* of such a scheme still haunts me."

"You mean another country picking up on it," Fowler said, "like maybe the former Soviet Union."

"That's possible, but let me toss out something for your consideration. Suppose a secret international cartel, a very powerful commission, is behind it all. We have suspected since the days of Hoover that there is literally a world government existing in the shadows, which uses its influence to monopolize the financial reservoirs and dominate the global military-industrial complex to sustain economic policies. Some think-tank wizards thought key players in George W's administration were controlled by this group, but they couldn't prove it. Anyway, Roosevelt believed both World Wars were essentially created by the underground activities of international bankers who financed national armies. So did Eisenhower."

Fowler gave him a nervous smile. "You don't believe that, do you Mr. Director?"

"Let's take it a step further," Brent said, ignoring the question. "In order to have world domination, they would have to go after the nations with an open society and a democratic form of government. And the other countries would fall in line because of the huge financial gain of their political leaders. It so happens that the missing people from outside our borders are all from countries favoring democracy."

Gillespie said, "You're raising the possibility that this mysterious commission or cartel planted children in democratic countries to be trained and programmed to some day rise up and take over? That sounds pretty far fetched."

"Not take over governments," Brent said. "Let's consider the possibility they were indoctrinated into every phase of a particular country's society and culture, its very consciousness if you will. And they became highly respected citizens, leaders with a broad national following. With the confidence of the people, they can now come out of the shadows to reveal a *planetary* government with the economic clout to literally bring dissenting countries to their knees. And with representatives from many countries, they could be headquartered anywhere and pulling the strings in the name of power and greed.

"It's my feeling that the missing people will soon surface and will issue some sort of proclamation, and there won't be a damn thing we can do about it. Fall in line or face a depression far worse than the great one."

"Is this all talk?" Voger asked.

The director's eyes narrowed.

"Sorry, sir. What I mean is, is this just hypothetical, or is there an action-position the Bureau is taking?"

"Justice doesn't want any part of this," Brent said, "at least until the attorney general is found. So I talked to Santanna at CIA. He's launching a deep probe, concentrating primarily in the European capitals. Any further comments?"

"We'll give some thought to your scenario," Gillespie said, "and we'll continue to check the computers for any red flags. In the meantime--"

Gillespie was interrupted by the ringing telephone. Brent answered, his secretary saying that Joseph Albright, Senator Obrey's former law partner, insisted on speaking to the director. Brent dismissed the men and took the call.

"Director Brent, you know that Senator Obrey and his wife were in my home the night they disappeared."

"Yes, Mr. Albright. My men were all over your

house after the agent reported they were missing."

"Well, even though your agents checked every room that evening, my wife just discovered this morning that their coats are still in our front closet. The agents must have thought they were ours. With the kind of weather we've been having, I find it rather peculiar they would leave without their coats. Oh, Helen Obrey's purse was there, too. I took the liberty of looking inside."

"And?"

"There's a small makeup kit and a wallet containing her driver's license, an American Express card, and several hundred dollars. It would appear to me, Director Brent, that they didn't leave the premises on their own. At precisely eight o'clock the telephone rang and my wife answered it in the kitchen. It was for the senator and we left him and Helen alone. When we returned a few minutes later, they were gone."

"That's all in the report, Mr. Albright."

"Yes, but our conversation with the agents did not focus on the possibility that one or more persons entered the back door, immobilized them, and took them to a waiting car on the side entrance to the street."

"They may not have discussed that with you, but it certainly entered their minds. However, the idea was quickly dropped when no footprints were found in the snow on your back steps, or in the backyard. And no fresh ones in the front, I might add."

"Oh. But how do you explain the coats and purse?"

"Right now I have no rational explanation." Brent hung up and stared into space.

Chapter 13

Jason Miller pulled a color photo from his wallet. "Remember this?"   Robert Ames took it, smiled. "It's the group picture that Alexandria took of us one summer when we were in high school."

"And do you remember anything significant about that gathering?"

Robert's smile faded. "I hadn't thought about that in years." Every detail of the experience suddenly began playing on the screen of his mind.

***

"Where's Lisa?" Robert asked Carlton Matthews.

"She saw a dog when we were coming back from the beach. I think she's trying to catch it."

Robert walked to the edge of the woods and called for several minutes. No answer. "It's almost dark," Robert said. "Maybe we should catch *her* before she gets lost in the thick underbrush. I'll get flashlights." He wasn't concerned about Lisa, but a rescue game would be fun. He liked playing in the forest after dark. Returning, he asked if anyone else wanted to join the search party, adding before they could speak, "And remember, I'm in charge because it's my idea. Now, do I have any volunteers?" All hands were raised. "Great, but someone should stay behind in case we miss her and she comes back."

"I'll keep watch here," Claudia said.

Robert passed out the flashlights. "Okay, let's split up. Jason, Carlton and Curtis and I will spread out and move into the trees above the beach road. Frank, Burton, Frederick and Julius will do the same on the other side of the island. Merriam and Simon will take the middle. All right, let's go."

Ten teenagers, still wearing their bathing suits, began the search from their assigned positions, everyone hollering Lisa's name. She didn't hear them. As Robert learned later, the dog she was following, left there by a tourist Lisa thought, had led her on a merry chase through the forest. She was almost at the dock on the other side of the island before she realized where she was.

Lisa knew the last ferry had left hours before, another one not until morning. What she didn't know was that two eighteen year olds, Jack Mead and Tommy Cartright, had missed the ferry and were sitting in a car at the dock drinking beer. They saw her when she came out of the trees, the brightness of the moonlight giving her high visibility as she took the beach road back toward her friends.

Lisa heard the sound of the engine starting, looked back, saw the car coming her way. She knew she was in danger and had two choices. Try to lose them in the trees, or jump down the incline to the beach. For some reason, which she understood moments later, she decided to keep running on the road.

The car was moving faster now, and as she sprinted around a sharp curve she saw something standing a few yards ahead in the middle of the road. It was the small white dog she'd been following in the woods.

She screamed. "Car! Get away!" It didn't move. Within seconds her hands were on the animal, shoving it to the side toward the incline.

But it was an instant too late for Lisa. She heard the squealing tires, then felt the car slam into her, throwing her against the pavement, the left front tire rolling over her upper back. Thoughts flew rapidly through her mind. *Can't happen...no!* Then darkness came.

Chapter 14

The two teenagers got out of the car. They were wearing jeans and t-shirts, sandals. They saw Lisa's head and shoulders protruding from under the car. She was on her stomach, arms stretched out in front of her, blood flowing in a thin line from her mouth.

As they reached down to pull her out, a voice said, "Don't touch her." They looked up to see two boys jumping down from the embankment, another two running toward them, trying to shield their eyes from the headlights.

"Look, it was an accident," Tommy said, fear in his eyes. "All of a sudden she was there in the road. There wasn't anything we could do."

"Yeah," Jack said shaking his head, "I jammed on the brakes, couldn't stop in time. Do you know her?"

As Carlton slowly pulled Lisa to where he could lift her, Jason and Curtis looking on, Robert said, "We're family. Now tell us what you were doing out here. You were trying to catch her, weren't you."

"Look man," Jack said, "we missed the ferry and were just having a beer when we saw this girl come out of the woods. We got curious and started following her. You'd have done the same thing in our shoes." He whispered, "Is...is she dead?"

Robert studied them for a moment. Clean-cut high schoolers he thought, didn't appear to be troublemakers. "Both of you wait here," he said. He took the keys out of the ignition and ran down to the beach where Carlton had carried Lisa. He was sitting on the sand holding her in his arms, the other two boys standing beside them. The small white dog was watching nearby.

"What's the situation?" Robert asked.

"She's all right," Carlton said. "We're just trying to figure out how to play this."

"They saw the tire tracks on her back," Curtis said, "and the blood from her mouth indicating internal bleeding. We can't let them see her walk away."

Robert said, "Let me handle it."

"Show them where they can turn around, and get them out of here," Jason said.

The two teens were sitting on the ground, heads in their hands. They looked up as Robert approached with a flashlight. "We're not going to call the police," he said, "because from all indications it was, as you explained, an accident. Fortunately, the girl was not injured seriously."

Jack said, his voice low, "I thought I'd killed her. Are you sure she's going to be okay?"

"I'm sure. Be glad you have soft tires and she's in excellent physical condition. She could have been killed. Let this be a lesson to you. The next time you think about following a girl, a woman, with the idea you're going to force yourself on her, think again. What goes around comes around, and whenever you hurt someone else, you become nothing but a target yourself.

Maybe not in the same way, but as sure as I'm standing here, I'll guarantee you'll get yours. Do you understand what I'm saying?"

Tommy said, "You look younger than we are, but you talk like my father."

"You didn't answer my question."

They both nodded. "We hear you," Tommy said, "but what you got to understand is that we were just playing around, didn't mean any harm. And thanks for not calling the cops."

"Yeah, neither one of us has been in trouble before." Jack said. "I guess we just kind of lost it, drank too much beer. Please tell her for me I'm really sorry. I've got a girl friend back home, and I know how I'd feel if something happened to her. Thank God it didn't end up a lot worse tonight. "

"You might spend the rest of the night doing just that," Robert said. "Now I would suggest you get back to the dock and take the first ferry in the morning." He gave Jack the keys. "Back up about fifty yards and you'll find a turnaround. Now get out of here."

Robert ran back to the others. Lisa was standing, Carlton holding her arm. "They're on their way," Robert said. He looked at Lisa. "You're okay?"

She nodded. "I'm sorry about this. I wasn't concentrating."

Jason smiled. "It was the dog. Your thinking led you to save the dog, but instead of seeing you *and* the dog safely out of the way, your mind focused only on the animal. A temporary loss of faculty. I think we all learned a valuable lesson tonight, including those boys."

Lisa stretched her body, said, "I don't think Alexandra needs to know about this."

Carlton laughed. "She will. Bet on it."

***

Robert returned the photograph to Jason, saying, "I think it's kind of appropriate that Lisa is holding the dog in the picture, a reminder for her."

"Yeah, she wanted to take him home with her. Couldn't figure out how to do it, so he stayed on the island with Alexandria. Lisa named him Star."

Robert smiled. "Dog Star."

Chapter 15

Keri was standing just inside the door of Vincenzo's when Phillip Lansing arrived. "Sorry I'm late," he said, "had to make a couple of phone calls. When you're out of a job you've got to renew your contacts."

Her eyes widened. "You were fired?"

"Nope, I quit. I'm ready to do something else anyway. Being put in a straightjacket doesn't appeal to my journalistic senses." He saw the maitre'd waiting nearby in his standard evening attire--white shirt, black bow tie and black trousers. To Phillip, he looked more Greek than Italian. "Hello, Arturo."

"Ah, Ms. Winslow and Mr. Manning, good to see you again. Please follow me." He showed them to a corner table and took their drink order: Scotch and water for Phillip, a glass of the house chardonnay for Keri. "Loren will be your waiter," Arturo said. "I'll let him tell you about tonight's specials." He moistened his lips. "I recommend the delicious roasted veal with grapes."

Phillip nodded, and as Arturo scooted away, Phillip was about to speak, paused and stared at Keri. A beautiful woman. Curves of golden hair gently framing her face, an added touch of eye makeup giving her a more sensual look, the deep blue knit dress matching the color of her eyes.

"What!"

"Just admiring how beautiful you are tonight."

Keri tilted her head. "Thank you. With all you have on your mind, I consider that a real compliment. Now tell me what's going on. Anything to do with the missing people and those two men being killed today? We both know whoever pulled the trigger thought Senator Obrey was in the car."

He shook his head, smiled. "The belle of the ball dons her news woman hat. Okay, it all ties together in some way. Despite the murders, the big question is *where are they*? But with all the spin control in high places, we're blocked at every turn. It's a damn cover-up, and I knew I couldn't get to the bottom of it as long as I was a part of the protective shell." He paused. "Have you learned anything while I've been gone?"

Keri waited to answer until the drinks were served and water poured, her gaze lifted to the framed photos of Italian-American celebrities on the wall. Soft accordion music in the background and a hint of garlic in the air added to the ambience of her favorite restaurant. She took a sip of wine. "To answer your question, not a lot, and part of what I've heard is off-the-wall ridiculous." She told him about the two calls she received from the same unknown man, repeated the conversation with the bartender, adding the information from Sigler concerning the burglaries.

"I hadn't heard about the break-ins." He tasted his drink, thinking. "And what you got from the bartender, well, the kidnapping theory just isn't realistic. And forget the sci-fi fantasy. I heard a few years ago Congress had appropriated funds for the development of a weapon that changed the physical structure of a target into pure energy, but the prototype never worked. What your caller said is closer to the truth."

"That's my feeling."

A plumpish elderly man with gray moustache approached the table, smiled. "As usual, we have our delightful specials. First--"

Phillip held up a hand. "Give us a few more minutes. We're in no hurry tonight."

The waiter nodded and walked away. Phillip noticed a couple at another table watching them, lowered his voice. "The disappearances had to be planned by the individuals themselves. It's the *why* that eludes me. I can't figure it out. When I told my chief I was going to investigate it further, he said no, that all the so-called missing people were never missing in the first place. The network chairman said they're all at a top-secret planning conference in Canada, and attributed the rumor to an early-on communications hitch involving the police. And he probably thinks the Obrey car being shot up and the killing of those two thugs was only an isolated incident."

"In other words," Keri said, "the network higher-ups say there's no story. You think there is. I agree. It's not everyday key people pick up and run. You wanted to pursue it further, and that's why you resigned."

He bit his lip. "You're partly right. While I can't speak for the others, Secretary of State Carlton

Matthews and I have been close personal friends since college. I was in one of his classes. I guess he took a liking to me and we started bumming around together on the weekends. He's about ten years older than I am, but that didn't seem to matter at the time.

"Anyway, what I'm trying to say is that if I've ever known anyone with total integrity and devotion to his country, it's him. He's not about to *run* from anything." He glanced at the ceiling. "No, Carlton is on to something, and I've got a gut feeling that whatever it is it's big, *very* big."

"I take it, from the tone of your voice, that you think the situation may be ominous." She thought of Chance's mention of danger and probing too far, and the dream.

"Could be. Anything unknown and as bizarre as this is has a way of tapping into some deep primordial fears." Seeing a slight tremble of her shoulders, he said, "Enough of this. Let's order." As he was trying to spot the waiter, the phone in his coat pocket rang. He pulled it out and answered.

"Phillip, I know you recognize my voice but don't use my name, and from the background noise I'm assuming you're not alone."

"You're correct on both counts." He leaned back in his chair.

"I want you to catch the United flight for Chicago leaving at ten twenty-five tonight. When you arrive at O'Hare, stay in the terminal and board the seven a.m. flight to Seattle where you will take a cab to the Alexis

Hotel. A room has been reserved in your name. After you check in, call the desk and ask for Ms Day's room. Tell no one and don't ask any questions now. Your ticket will be at the United ticket counter. I'll see you tomorrow."

"Right, tomorrow." Hearing the line go dead, he replaced the phone. "Keri, I apologize. I've got to catch a flight and don't have a lot of time. You're going to have to eat without me."

"Who was that on the phone?"

"I can't say."

"Look, Phillip, I think you know me well enough to trust me. And you're no longer in the news business, remember? If this has anything to do with the missing people, we could work together and--"

"I have to do it alone." He reached over and touched her face. "I'm sorry. My instructions were very clear. This is a solo job, but I'll promise you I'll tell you everything when I can, and you'll have a leg up on the others. In the meantime, don't say anything to anyone regarding the call. I'll be out of town for a few days, so just wait until you hear from me. Okay?"

She smiled. "I don't seem to have a choice."

"Afraid not." He stood to speak to the approaching waiter. "My friend will be dining alone. I've been called away on business, and I'm sure she's ready to order." He walked around and kissed Keri on the cheek. "Thanks for understanding. I'll call you when I can."

She waited until Phillip left and said to the waiter, "Another time. I suddenly lost my appetite."

Keri paid the check for the drinks and hurried to the door to see Phillip drive away in his red SUV. Moments later she was following at a distance, knew he was heading for his apartment on Virginia Avenue.

The snow had stopped, the low overhanging clouds giving way to tiny specs of pale fire in the clear night sky. Colder though, Keri thought as she adjusted the heater. Seeing Phillip turn into the parking garage of the complex, she stopped and backed the Honda half a block and parked on the opposite side of the street, lights off. She would wait here and follow him to the airport.

She thought about her dates with Phillip during the past few months and smiled. For all his professional sophistication in front of the camera, in real life he was laid back with few pretensions about himself, or his job. She was fond of him and was glad Al was no longer a part of her life.

Keri had been engaged to Dr. Alfred Gentry, an orthopedic surgeon in Baltimore, when she was a TV reporter there. As his uncalled for jealousy became more apparent, she broke off the engagement and applied for the news slot she heard was opening up at WTCX in D.C.

To escape the continuing harassment by Al--early morning and late night phone calls--she quit her job and moved to Washington before a final offer came through. It turned out to be the right decision. Erickson, the news director, wanted her and she was free of Al. That was three years ago, and she hadn't seen or heard from him since. And she loved her work, at least most of the time.

Her thoughts were broken by a taxi rounding the corner and stopping at the entrance to the building. She observed Phillip hurrying down the steps with a hangerbag and briefcase. Knowing their destination, she hung back a few seconds and followed at a discreet distance.

When the cab stopped at the United entrance, she pulled ahead, parked at the curb and popped the trunk open. If a cop was watching, he'd think she was letting someone out, luggage to be retrieved. No cop in sight. Too cold. She left the motor running, trunk up, and ran into the terminal.

Phillip was in line at the ticket counter. She stepped behind a pillar. When it was his turn, she heard him say, "You have a ticket for Phillip Lansing, Seattle by way of Chicago."

The agent reached in a drawer, removed the envelope. "Yes, Mr. Lansing. It's a pleasure having you fly with us." He extended his hand. "I met Dan Rather once, but my wife says you're the best, should be an anchorman."

Phillip smiled, shook his hand. "Thank her for me."

"Any luggage?"

"Only what I'm carrying."

"You'll be leaving from Gate Forty, boarding in about thirty minutes. Enjoy your trip."

Keri watched as Phillip headed toward the security check, then walked back to her car. She saw a cop half a block down, his back to her. She moved the car forward to the end of the unloading zone, figured she had enough time to take care of business. She went back into the terminal and checked on the next available flight to Seattle at the United counter. There was one scheduled for eight-fifteen the next morning by way of Salt Lake City. She purchased the ticket then stepped outside to use her cell phone.

Erickson answered on the first ring. "Randall, this is Keri. I think I may be on to something regarding the missing VIPs, but I've got to go out of town to check it out."

The voice was brusk. "What have you got and where are you going? Spell it out."

She hesitated. "All I can say is that I've got a good lead, but the source has to remain anonymous."

"What kind of a lead?"

"I can't tell you that either. Just give me a few days, and if I don't bring you a ratings-boosting story, you can find a replacement for me and I'll leave quietly."

Erickson was silent for a moment. He knew Keri Winslow was trophy quality and was considering making her the late evening anchor with Jerry Schuster. He also knew she was a news hound and would bust her buns to get the story behind the story, something the others didn't think about. "All right, you've got three days, seventy-two hours. That's it. And keep the expenses down."

With the disconnect, Keri went home to pack and

get a few hours sleep, making one stop on the way to pick up a couple of necessities.

After talking to Keri, Erickson called Chance Patton to tell him she was going to be out of town on assignment, a follow-up on the missing people story, and he would have a different co-anchor for a few days.

Patton turned off the television, paced the small living room thinking, knew what he had to do. He picked up the phone and called Tony Voger's home number. "Keri Winslow knows something about the disappearances. Randall Erickson called me, said she's leaving town soon to check it out."

"What's the source?"

"She wouldn't tell Randall, but my guess is Phillip Lansing. She was going to have dinner with him tonight. Maybe they're working together."

By midnight, FBI agents were watching both apartments.

Chapter 16

As the plane reached cruising altitude, Phillip was deep in thought about the dramatic turn he felt his life was taking. Unemployed, limited resources, at least for the long haul, flying to meet an old friend. So damn mysterious and secretive on the phone.

He and Carlton Matthews had both grown up in Concord, Massachusetts, but met for the first time in Carlton's history class at Northeastern University in Boston. Despite the student-teacher relationship, they became friends. Since Carlton didn't own a car, Phillip offered to drive whenever his friend needed a lift. As the Christmas holidays drew near Phillip remembered asking Carlton if he would like a ride to Concord. He declined the invitation, saying his parents had moved away. Phillip's father told him later that people in the community were puzzled when Edward Matthews and his wife suddenly closed their art gallery and moved away a few weeks after Carlton enrolled in college. When Phillip casually questioned Carlton about it, he changed the subject.

After graduation, Phillip landed a job as a reporter with the *Boston Globe*. A stint with the *New York Times* and *Newsweek* followed, finally jumping into electronic media with the network, the past two years as White House correspondent. He had kept in contact with Carlton and was as shocked as everyone when his friend was named Secretary of State, even more so when the Senate gave its quick approval.

Carlton simply didn't fit the mold, the "requirements" some said, to head up the Department of State as chief advisor on foreign affairs. He was an easygoing small towner with the storied demeanor of New England academia, the polar opposite of senior cabinet members in previous administrations with their mainline social standing and worldly airs.

Phillip thought again about the phone call. *This has got to be an international problem, but why call me? If he wanted to leak a story, he's got ears out there who specialize in that sort of thing. And why Seattle?*

Phillip closed his eyes and searched for possible answers hiding in the recesses of his mind. He thought about dinner at the Matthews home only a few evenings before. Eve, a small woman with blonde hair and blue eyes on a cherub face, served a sumptuous meal of her own creation. They talked until well past midnight. Phillip remembered being confused at times by enigmatic statements injected by Carlton that were out of context, comments on quantum physics and virtual images that didn't make sense. His questions as to the meaning of the remarks were not acknowledged, and when Phillip continued to probe he was ignored, the talk returning to the subject at hand.

Deciding to get some sleep, he pushed the button and reclined the seat. Taking several deep breaths to relax, he was almost in the twilight state when he began to remember some of the idle talk about Carlton and his family. Some said he could play classical piano, but had never taken a lesson. Others had whispered that the family practiced witchcraft, a neighbor swearing she had seen Carlton bring a dead cat back to life. That report added to the talk about all the animals, including some wild ones, being attracted to their home.

Phillip hadn't paid much attention because back then everyone talked about everyone. He'd heard the high school English teacher was a heroin addict, the Baptist minister a homosexual, and that the local banker's wife hadn't committed suicide but had been murdered by her husband. He smiled. People just didn't have anything better to do than gossip, the malady of small town America.

But then he recalled particular conversations with Carlton at college and the night an intensely bright light mysteriously appeared around him as they walked across the campus. Phillip had dismissed it then as some sort of reflection and a vivid imagination.

Now he wondered, and suddenly all the disjointed pieces began to fit together. *The Club of Apollo*. He sat up straight. *No!* He tried to shake off the realization, but it remained, a dark picture forming in his mind. Maybe Carlton had been giving him veiled hints, inferences, keys to the unraveling of what had to be one of the most ancient of mysteries, a tremulous unknown that continued to be fearfully controversial to this day. Phillip felt the hair rising on the back of his neck.

***

Benton Fowler entered the FBI Director's office.

"Wallace, one of our agents in New York found a message telephoned to Ambassador Livingston Vance at the UN. She wasn't in her office at the time and a temporary clerk took the call and wrote down the message, said she gave it to the ambassador when she came in. The agent found it in her desk." He handed the paper to the director. "Maybe you can figure it out."

Brent read it aloud. "Sigma wary, domestic only. Awkward state drawing as chore power naught of varlet eta-kin moving to erase dicga osterkind. Suggest immediate exit with synthesis in sealth islet." He looked up. "What the hell is this?"

Fowler smiled. "I don't know, but it may be what triggered the disappearances. I had our decoders take a look at it and they're still working. I also sent a copy over to the cryptographers at CIA. Haven't heard back yet."

"Our people don't have any ideas?"

"Well, Agent Young said sigma and eta were letters in the Greek alphabet, 'varlet' is an archaic word meaning scoundrel, but he had no idea what dicga or osterkind meant, could only assume they were to be eliminated, erased. He couldn't figure out sealth either, except that it was obviously an unknown island."

Brent frowned, shook his head. "And chore power naught?"

"Well, chore is a job or task. It could mean it's all been for nothing."

The director glanced at the message again. "Sigma wary, domestic only. Sigma is the eighteenth Greek letter. Eighteen wary, cautious, suspicious. But counting husbands and wives, there are twenty-four people missing, not eighteen."

"Eighteen is referring to something else," Fowler said.

Brent looked at his calendar. "Like maybe the day of the month. The eighteenth is day after tomorrow." He paused. "No, that's not it."

Fowler said, "I agree. Whatever eighteen means, 'domestic only' could relate to people who live here in the United States."

"And it's saying something is about to happen, trouble is brewing, as someone or something evil is preparing to eliminate a designated group of Americans."

"You're right," Fowler said. "Basically it's a warning, and again the key word seems to be Sigma. If we could figure that out, maybe the rest would fall in place."

"Maybe the message is too simple, the answer right here, but we just can't see it. I'll have Millie take a look at it. She once taught a course in semantics at Georgetown University and might be able to shed some light on what the caller was really saying."

Chapter 17

It was a beautiful sunny day with temperature in the fifties when Phillip's plane touched down. He hadn't visited Seattle before, had heard it always rained and was dark and damp in the winter season. He was pleased by the exception.

He followed Carlton's instruction to take a cab. The driver, an elderly Asian man, was quiet during the twenty minute drive to the city, except to volunteer that the Alexis was a small and intimate hotel listed in the *National Register of Historic Places.*

"Fine," Phillip said as his mind tried to focus on what he was going to say to his friend. He finally decided he would simply tell him what he thought he knew and let Carlton pick it up from there, to either deny or affirm. Then he thought of Keri, and was glad she wasn't with him. This could get sticky, and with her instinct for a story, she could mess things up fast.

The cab pulled up in front of the three story building. Phillip paid the fare and was quickly escorted to the front desk, then to his room on the second floor by a Joe College type who never stopped talking about the magic and beauty of the Emerald City. Phillip thanked him for the Visitors Bureau hype, tipped him and picked up the phone as the door closed. He asked for Ms. Day's room. A woman answered.

"This is Phillip Lansing--"

"Hello, Phillip. Thank you for coming." Her voice was soft and melodious. "My name is Alexandria Day, and I am working with your friend on the project."

Phillip swallowed hard. "What project? All I know is what Carlton said on the phone last night, and that wasn't much. Is he there with you?"

"No, I'm to take you to him. Look at your watch. In one hour come to my room. It's number three-fifteen. I'll answer your questions then. Phillip, I look forward to meeting you in person."

"Look Ms--"

"I will see you in one hour. Goodbye Phillip."

He replaced the receiver and sat on the bed. He would have to play it differently with this woman, not revealing any suspicions, just ask what was going on and let her talk. He wondered about the relationship between Carlton and Alexandria Day, and where he might be hiding now. And was Eve with him? And the others?

***

The twenty-four men and women were seated on two rows in a small auditorium, a heavy-set middle-age man standing before them. He was speaking English with a German accent.

"Those from the other countries are waiting in the departure lounge. When I join them we will return to our posts and attempt to restore some semblance of order. But first, a quick report. As you know, the disappearances have caused panic in the streets of Bonn, London, Paris, Rome, and Athens. Concern is also evident in Canada, Australia, Japan, and the Scandinavian countries. From our monitors here in America, we are hearing of a few organized demonstrations against the government, and families packing up and leaving Washington. A special session of the UN has been called.

"However, I have been assured by our colleagues that the darkest hour has passed, at least here in America, primarily due to the efforts of President Underwood. He has been on radio and television telling the American people that a full disclosure of the whereabouts of the missing people will be made within seventy-two hours. I have no idea what he will say, and I'm sure he doesn't either at this time.

"You should also know that a new group of twelve in the U.S. has been alerted. They will soon be contacted and asked to assume the positions you have held. You may be sure they will be equally effective in furthering our objectives. Now I must leave. I am expected in my office in Bonn in the morning."

As he walked away, Congressman Julius Andrews said, "He's done a splendid job in Germany, but I'm pleased we were given the U.S. assignment."

Senator Claudia Ferguson smiled. "But you're not going to protest going home. Right?"

"I've greatly enjoyed living in America," Andrews said with a nod, "and I'll carry many wonderful memories with me. But with all that's happened, I'm ready to go."

"That will probably be tomorrow," Carlton

Matthews said. "I heard from Alexandria and she's returning late this afternoon with Phillip Lansing."

General Craig held his hands up. "What on earth for? I mean, why is she bringing a TV reporter here?"

"It was my idea," Carlton said, "and Alexandria agreed. I felt we needed someone to act as a channel for us, to create a sense of understanding among the American people of our purpose for being here."

"What if he rejects being a part of our efforts?" the General asked.

"I've been working on him very subtly for over twenty years. With Alexandria explaining everything as only she can do, I think he'll come on board."

"Please let me know when she arrives," the General said.

Carlton nodded and left the auditorium with his wife, Eve, and Robert and Paula Ames.

***

Eric Turnell, an FBI agent with the Seattle field office, observed the departing passengers. Using a faxed photo he spotted Keri as she entered the main terminal. He followed her rental car to the hotel and parked on the street. An agent in Washington, D.C. was still watching Phillip's apartment.

On the recommendation of her seat companion on the plane, Keri called the Sorrento from the airport and was able to book a room. When she checked in, she asked if Phillip Lansing was registered. The clerk's computer produced a negative. Once in her room, she pulled out the Yellow Pages and started calling the hotels. The voice at the Alexis said yes, and rang the room. Keri immediately hung up.

First things first, she thought as she removed the black wig from her suitcase. It was cheap and floozy looking, but the best she could find in a hurry last night. She washed her face and put her hair up, then changed into sweat pants, baggy sweater, a blue nylon windbreaker and running shoes.

Slipping on the wig and oversized dark glasses, she looked at herself in the mirror. With the lumpish sweater under the jacket, she appeared heavier. She smiled. The perfect disguise--a short-haired brunette with hidden eyes ready to go jogging to get back in shape.

Deciding a purse didn't look right with the outfit, she folded her money and tucked the bills into a pocket, along with her room key. It had occurred to her to forget the rental car, maps, and finding places to park. She would take a taxi to the Alexis and decide what to do next when the time came.

As she got into the taxi in the fountain courtyard of the Sorrento, the FBI agent parked on the street smiled. He had been fooled by wigs and disguises before, but not this time.

***

Phillip knocked on the door of room three-fifteen. When it opened, he could only stare, speechless. The exquisitely beautiful woman standing before him took his breath away. She had long dark hair and Eurasian eyes, and was wearing a white Grecian-style dress that accented her stunning figure. She smiled and offered her hand. "Phillip, I have heard so much about you. It's a pleasure to finally meet you."

He shook her hand, said, "Ms. Day, I--"

"Call me Alexandria. Please come in." She pointed to a love seat and chairs grouped by the window in the suite's large living room. "May I offer you a cup of coffee? I had a pot brought up."

"That would be fine. Black." He watched as she moved gracefully to the small dining table and filled two cups. "Alexandria, where is Carlton?"

"He is on one of the San Juan Islands. We will take the ferry over later. He and Eve are expecting us for dinner." She handed him the coffee. "Please sit down. I know you must have many questions, and Carlton has asked me to do what I can to contribute to your understanding."

He chose one of the club chairs. "Understanding of what?"

She sat on the love seat across from him, her black eyes sparkling. He watched as she set the cup on the table and leaned back. "The understanding of our mission, and what we will accomplish."

"I'm assuming this all has a beginning somewhere. Why don't you start there."

"To use your word, there have been many beginnings. The current effort is number eighteen, and that is why it is called Sigma." She smiled. "We number our missions by the letters in the Greek alphabet. Sigma was initiated in nineteen fifty-four and continues to this day." She got up and brought him a pad and pen. "Here, you'll need to make notes."

For over an hour she talked about the Sigma plan, pausing at each interruption to answer his questions with candor and clarity. Finally she said, "I think you can now see the essential ingredients of the overall operation."

He stood and stepped to the window, his gaze fixed on the gardens below. "I thought something like this might be behind the disappearances, but the enormity of it all is hard to believe."

"Sometimes we do not want to know the truth."

He turned to face her. "Alexandria, what in the name of God am I supposed to do with this?"

"We want you to write a book, to be published at the appropriate time. Its purpose will be to prepare people for what is to come."

"The price of such revelations is too high. The consequences of a book reporting everything you've said could be cataclysmic. And why me?"

"Carlton has had you in mind as the chronicler since you were in college. And yes, for a time the truth may be disturbing, but that will pass as people understand and accept the inevitable."

He looked into her eyes. "And if I say no, can I walk out of here and fly back to Washington?"

She smiled. "Phillip, Sigma is rising to confront the challenge before us, and we are past the point of no return. Concerning your assignment, it is yours because you are the chosen one."

"Theologically, that means favored by God. I don't think so."

***

Keri, pretending to window shop, had been watching the hotel from across the street for more than an hour. She finally decided to go into the hotel, buy a newspaper for cover, and keep an eye out for him while sitting in the lobby. It wasn't necessary. There they were, Phillip and a woman leaving the hotel and getting into a waiting car.

Keri ran to the taxi parked at the curb, told the driver to follow the white Continental.

He laughed, saying he had always wanted a passenger to speak those words. "Just like in the movies."

"Yeah," Keri said, "but so far I'm just a bit player."

She leaned back, suddenly feeling a sense of guilt for following Phillip to Seattle. She wished now that she had stayed in Washington and waited for his call.

As the cab paused for a light, she glanced out the window at the white Victorian home with the large porch swing. It brought back a childhood memory. She closed her eyes, thinking about the times she and her mother sat together in the swing on late afternoons reading poetry. She could almost see the flowering dogwood and the wild azaleas, feel the warm, gentle breeze of those soothing, nurturing days between winter and summer.

Keri had grown up in Charlottesville, Virginia in what would be called an average family, but she didn't feel ordinary. Her father owned and published a weekly newspaper and her mother taught school. From Keri's perspective, they were as well off as anyone. She'd liked the sense of independence she had felt during her adolescence. An only child, her parents gave her a long leash. She responded with a maturity beyond her years.

She went to work for the paper the summer after her junior year in high school, and her gossipy "Around the Town" column became an instant hit. The next year she tried her hand at investigative reporting. She followed two former students suspected of dealing drugs and secretly photographed them selling cocaine near the campus. She turned the pictures over to the police and reported on the arrests with a front page story with her by-line. Encouraged by her parents, she enrolled at the University of Virginia and majored in radio-television. Her mother died the month after Keri's graduation.

She treasured those times when her mother read to her, usually from Ralph Waldo Emerson, her favorite poet. So mystical, yet so beautiful were the words as a few lines from Emerson's *Voluntaries* came to mind.

And their coming triumph hide
In our downfall or our joy:
They reach no term, they never sleep,
In equal strength through space abide...
Speak it firmly, these are gods,
All are ghosts beside.

She sat up in the seat, wondering why pieces of this particular narrative were suddenly remembered.

Chapter 18

FBI Special Agent Tony Voger closed the door to his office and returned to his high-back leather desk chair, his head in his hands. Voger had been a credit to the Bureau for nearly twenty years, and with his last promotion was in line for the Deputy Director's job. And now he was about to throw it all away. Anger and fear were gripping him, yet there was no way out, no alternative.

Unless he could make everything appear as though it was best for the country, convince the director, maybe even the president that America was about to be destroyed. For the sake of national security he did what he had to do. He hit the desk with his fist, his thoughts flowing. Going directly to the American people could be the solution. There were enough of them out there who will believe me. If necessary, we'll rally together in a massive rebellion to put this country back in sane hands. He looked back at the picture of his mother on the credenza. *And my darling, you'll be our standard bearer. Your cup of sorrow will be held up for all to see. I won't let you down.*

As he let out a deep breath, the phone rang. It was Agent Eric Turnell calling from his cell phone. He said, "I'm following the cab that picked up Keri Winslow. It appears they're heading for the Washington State Ferry at Anacortes. Probably going across to the San Juan

Islands."

"Is she alone?"

"Yeah, and all decked out in a black wig. I think she was watching for someone at the hotel. When a man and a woman left in a white Continental, Winslow quickly flagged down a cab to follow it. I've been sticking close."

"Did you get a look at the couple?" Voger asked.

"A dark-haired woman, young. And a tall slender man, brown hair and probably in his forties. He looked familiar."

"It's got to be Phillip Lansing. He's not in his apartment and I figure he left town last night before we began the surveillance. Now we know why Winslow flew to Seattle. She dates Lansing, and he's a close friend of Carlton Matthews. Lansing is probably one of them and knows where they're all hiding. And Winslow thinks she has a story."

"What are my instructions once we get to the ferry?"

"Give me a description of the situation as you see it."

"The cab will drop Winslow off and she'll board as a walk-on passenger. I'll take my car on and stay close to the Continental. The ferry from Anacortes stops at different islands-Lopez, Shaw, Orcas, and Friday Harbor. When the Lincoln leaves the ferry I will too. Since Winslow will be on foot, I'll offer her a ride and try to get some information out of her while tailing Lansing. "

Voger didn't comment immediately. Finally he said, voice low, "Listen carefully. As soon as I hang up, call Agents Ruter and Kreps and instruct them to alert every member of our group throughout the Pacific Northwest and to have sufficient choppers standing by. Tell them you'll call again as soon as you know the right island, and to use the Minutemen code for the scramble. It's been programmed in the computer and the other agents in the field offices will think you are all on an undercover assignment concerning the militias. No questions will be asked.

"Make sure you get Winslow into your car. Then when you determine where Lansing and the other woman are going, get your team in the air. At that point call me. Oh, and one more thing. At the first opportunity take out Keri Winslow."

"Is that really necessary?"

"It is. We can't leave any witnesses around to talk, particularly reporters."

"What about Lansing?"

"He'll be terminated with the others. You'll get them all at one time. Now, are you clear on everything?"

Agent Turnell frowned. "You're the boss."

***

Keri turned the collar up on her jacket as she stood by the railing out of Phillip's sight and enjoyed the beautiful views of the small islands and abundant sea life. She reasoned he would stay in the car to avoid the risk of being seen and recognized. Her attention was drawn to a couple laughing nearby. Noticing their bicycles it suddenly dawned on her that she would have no transportation once on the island. Maybe she could rent something, either two wheel or four. After going this far she couldn't lose him.

When the ferry reached Lopez Island, the man and woman with the bicycles got off along with two of the cars. The white Continental remained. As they approached the next stop, Shaw Island, she heard an engine start up, saw the exhaust smoke of Phillip's car. The car behind it was also preparing to leave. She could see the driver talking on the telephone. She waited until both cars pulled away, watching the direction they were going, then ran to the store by the ferry dock. An elderly woman behind the counter was the single occupant.

"Hi," Keri said. "Do you by any chance have a vehicle I could rent?"

The woman smiled. "I'm sorry, no." She glanced up to see a man in a dark brown sport coat and open collar walk in. He was wearing dark glasses and a hat.

"Not even a bicycle?" She laughed. "Even a horse would do. I'd like to explore the island but my feet are killing me."

"The only transportation I can offer you is a small boat, but I wouldn't advise taking one out this late in the day. It will be dark in a little while, and not knowing your way around could be dangerous."

The man stepped up. "Perhaps I can be of service to the lady. I'm going to take some sunset pictures on the beach in County Park. My cameras are in the car, and you can see some of the island while I'm doing my work. We'll catch the last ferry back."

"I don't know."

He smiled. "Come on. You'll be perfectly safe. My wife, June, is already down there scouting things out. She came over earlier today. Excuse me for not introducing myself. I'm George Adams on assignment from the County Visitors Center."

"You might as well go with Mr. Adams," the woman said. "There's not much else on this island. No inns or tourist facilities, just an old building in the park, the pavilion. But you'll love the beautiful landscapes."

Keri asked, "What direction is the park?"

She pointed to the road the Continental had taken.

"All right, I guess it'll be okay." She thanked the woman and stepped through the door being held open by the man.

Phillip and his companion must be going to the park, but why did they choose this deserted place? They had to be meeting someone else. She'd try to slip away from Adams and his wife and look for that building.

Once in the car, Adams said, "You didn't give me your name."

"Oh, it's...Kay Winters."

"It's a pleasure meeting you, Ms. Winters. First time on the island?"

"Yes, I'm on vacation. My home is back east."

They were both silent as Keri observed the scenic beauty and the tranquility of the surroundings. Her mind turned to Phillip, hoping he would forgive her impulsiveness. She could see him sitting next to her, his smile and easy manner, the way he touched her hair, held her hand. She felt the beating of her heart, took a deep breath. She smiled broadly, the warmth of her feeling enveloping her.

Keri was jarred back to reality when Adams suddenly swung the car off the main road and made a winding path up a hillside through the trees, stopping near a narrow ravine. "What are we doing here?" she asked.

"I want to check the view from a higher elevation. I'll get my camera from the trunk."

Keri got out of the car and walked around to look down at the water. She didn't see him open a small bag and pull out a gun with a silencer. "It's so beautiful," she said. "And listen, the only sound are the birds."

He shoved the weapon into his belt and buttoned his coat. Closing the trunk, he said, "Keri Winslow, why don't you take off the wig. You're much more beautiful without it."

Keri froze. "Who are you?"

He produced his badge. "FBI Special Agent Eric Turnell. I guess we both had reasons to use another name."

The tension in her body eased. "Why didn't you say so in the first place?" She removed the wig and let her hair fall, tossing it with her fingers. "You must know that I'm following someone, trying to put the pieces together for a story."

"Yes, I know. Phillip Lansing."

She smiled. "You guys don't miss a trick. Look, whatever your reason for being here, let me tag along. And if we find Phillip, I'll tell him the truth. Maybe he won't be too angry with me."

The agent looked down and sighed. "I'm sorry, Ms. Winslow, but orders are orders." He opened his jacket and removed the gun and tightened the silencer.

Her eyes widened. "My God, what are you doing?" She stepped back and stumbled. Steadying herself, she said, "If you think I know anything you're wrong."

"Wrong place, wrong time. I'm sorry."

"Please...please don't..."

Turnell raised his arm. She turned away from him, put her hand over her eyes. He squeezed the trigger, and her arm dropped to the side. She seemed to straighten up, stand taller, not moving. He aimed again, but it wasn't necessary. For an instant she swayed, then she pitched forward, face down on the rocky slope. Turnell walked over and pushed her into the ravine, deep foliage partially obscuring the body. He broke off several cedar branches and dropped them down for complete concealment, covered the blood on the ground with fresh dirt. He picked up the wig and returned to the car, Eric Turnell had done his job and he felt sick.

He lit a cigarette, took a couple of deep drags and called Agent Ruter to bring in the team, instructing them to come in low over the water and land on the beach area near the park. "There's a pavilion on the other side of the island from the beach, a pretty steep ridge in between. It's the only building so they've got to be there."

The second call was to Voger. "The operation will take place on Shaw Island, and the choppers will be coming in after dark." Turnell reviewed the strategy and asked if there were any further instructions.

"What about Keri Winslow?"

"Terminated, the body properly disposed of."

"Anyone else see you on the island?"

"An old woman at the dock store."

"You know what to do."

"Yeah."

Chapter 19

Director Brent studied the message sent to the UN Ambassador again. *Sigma could be a reference to a fraternity,* he thought. *And fraternity is a brotherhood, a club, an alliance. Were the twelve united in a personal sort of way? Maybe so. Okay, they're being warned that the eta-kin, whoever they are, is about to eliminate the dicga osterkind, whatever that might be.*

As he threw up his hands in frustration, his secretary, Dori, entered the office delivering several faxed messages from the field offices. "I thought you ought to have these tonight," she said.

Brent scanned each page. "Good God! If these witnesses are reliable, I may have to rethink this whole thing." He shook his head and put the papers in his briefcase along with the coded message. He was saying goodnight to Dori when Gillespie came in.

"Wallace, you asked me to report on anything else we found in the top secret computer files for the year nineteen fifty-four."

Brent sat down, said wearily, "It's late, Gillespie, but let's hear it."

The assistant director forced a laugh. "I know this isn't the kind of thing you were looking for, but considering our storage capacity at that time you'd be amazed at how many files were identified with the prefix DL."

Speaking to Dori, Brent said, "DL is Dome Light, a code initiated in forty-seven to investigate UFO sightings."

"Just like on television," she said.

"Not really," Brent said. "The Bureau was never active in the project; we just monitored Air Force Intelligence. After Project Blue Book was discontinued in sixty-nine, investigations came under the authority of the Pentagon and carried out by the National Security Agency and Military Intelligence. It's not our bailiwick and I've never studied those files."

"You should have," Gillespie said, still grinning. "You would have seen how many people are unable to accept the realities of life. They have to invent something to give it meaning."

Dori asked, "Was fifty-four a significant year for so-called sightings?" Gillespie said, "According to what we have in the files, there were more alien-sighting claims in fifty-four than had ever been reported before in a single year, with thousands of newspaper items about UFOs. And that's when official Washington went into denial, believing that the mania over aliens was a greater danger to this country than the aliens themselves."

"Then the CIA got involved," Brent said. "They thought the Soviets might use the UFO furor as a way of sneaking their bombers into U.S. airspace. So in the interest of national security, the government issued an all encompassing official statement: there are no such things as UFOs, period."

Dori asked, "Is that your personal opinion, Mr. Director?"

Brent closed his briefcase, stood and reached for his coat. "Right now I don't have any opinions or answers about anything. Hopefully that will change by tomorrow."

***

Millie Brent met her husband at the door with a drink. "Thought you might need this," she said.

"Maybe more than one." He hung up his coat, took the bourbon and water and followed Millie into the living room. They sat on the couch in front of the fireplace, an artificial log burning brightly. "Guess I need to order in more wood."

Millie put her hand on his shoulder. "You've got enough on your mind right now. I picked up a box of the fake ones at the store. Not much heat, but they make a pretty fire. So how did it go today?"

"I wish you hadn't asked. Oh, before I forget it I want you to look at a scrambled message called in to the UN Ambassador's office." He got up and retrieved his briefcase. He removed the recently delivered faxes and placed them on the coffee table. Finally he found the sheet he was looking for. "With your background in reading the minds of people who write twisted meanings, maybe you can decipher this for me."

She looked at the paper. "Hmmm...Shouldn't be difficult. Give me some time to work on it and I'll see what I come up with."

Brent picked up one of the faxed messages from

the table. "Got this from the Chicago office today. Agent Bowers is heading a unit there that's trying to track down the parents of the missing people."

"Any luck?"

"Not a single stroke. Not only can't we find the parents of the twelve, but the families of their *spouses* don't seem to exist either. We talked to the Justice of the Peace who married Merriam Livingston and George Vance. The JP said that neither set of parents were in attendance, only a few friends. And when he asked about the parents, he was told that they had passed on."

"Well, tragic things happen and children sometimes do outlive their parents."

Brent continued. "Then we have Eve Matthews and Paula Ames. Eve, last name Austin, enrolled at Northeastern where she met Carlton Matthews. Six months later they were married. At about the same time, Paula Daniels shows up at Trinity University and starts going with Robert Ames."

"And they were soon married," Millie said.

"Right, and a similar story for the others, almost as if it was prearranged. School records show the parents' names of the spouses and place of residence, but the agents haven't been able to find anyone with those names ever living in those towns, and the addresses are phony."

"How strange!"

Brent took a swallow of his drink. "It gets more-so." He picked up the next message. "This is a report from an interview with Marge Freeman, a neighbor of the family that supposedly adopted Julius Andrews, the missing Speaker of the House. Mrs. Freeman said their little boy, Ronald by name, accidentally plunged a pitchfork into Julius when they were about ten years old. Ronald told his mother that Julius calmly removed the pitchfork from his belly, got up and ran home. When the Freeman's heard the story, they immediately went to Julius' house to check on him. He was fine. His parents said they used an old folk medicine remedy to heal his wounds and that he'd be going to school the next day."

"The boy could have suffered only minor flesh wounds," said Millie. "I wouldn't try to read too much into that story."

"Well then, how about these reports. By the time Frederick Craig, now *General* Craig, and Simon Ellenberg, *Justice* Ellenberg, reached the fifth grade, their IQ's were beyond the scale of measurement. And Merriam Livingston was caught by her third grade teacher doing advanced differential calculus in her workbook.

"And we found a friend of hers from early school years, a woman by the name of Debbie Collins, Debbie Turner back then. She said Merriam was a shy kid, but well-liked by her peers. The only thing strange she remembers is that Merriam forgot to bring her pajamas to a slumber party but later appeared with them on. When questioned, Merriam said she created them out of her mind. The kids got kind of spooked, until Merriam said she was just teasing, that she had the pajamas with her all the time. Mrs. Collins said she didn't and could never explain where they came from."

Millie grinned. "Any other weird stories?"

Brent thumbed through the sheath of papers. "Yeah, all sorts of strange happenings. Admiral Jessops supposedly running a world record hundred yard dash in high school, which was later attributed to a faulty stop-watch; Lisa Jackson, now *Senator* Lisa Cluse, saved a child from being run over by a car She was seen on one side of the street, and an instant later was on the other side with the little girl in her arms. And there are two reports of kids actually disappearing, I mean vanishing into thin air and reappearing seconds later."

"Who did *that*!"

According to old neighbors, it was Curtis O'Conner and Jason Miller, now senators. I've got an abnormal story for every one of them. Millie, those kids were more than just your everyday genius variety, more like mutants if you ask me, almost like a different breed of human. And think about it. One of them could have been living right next door. I just don't know who or what we're dealing with here."

Millie gathered the papers and placed them back in the briefcase. "That's enough for tonight. It's awfully late and I'm starving." She gave him a quick kiss on the lips. "Maybe you're one, too, a mutant I mean. I seem to remember you graduating at the top of your class at Harvard. Not bad for a cowpoke who wasn't really interested in studying law."

Chapter 20

Phillip, Alexandria, and Carlton and Eve Matthews had just finished dinner when they heard the sound of the approaching helicopters. Alexandria quickly ordered the sod-covered steel doors on the hill side closed. For more than an hour the group in the large underground structure watched the monitors as the men ran through the park and crossed the ridge and back in an intense search for their prey.

Seeing the battle dress of the men with FBI emblazoned front and back, Phillip said, "Our people, government agents, but they aren't just scouting the area. Not with those assault rifles."

"They're looking for us," Carlton said. "They want our people eliminated. I think you were followed."

Phillip shook his head. "The only person who knew I left the city was Keri Winslow, but she wouldn't tip the FBI, or anyone else for that matter."

"Maybe she trailed you here with the authorities shadowing her," Alexandria said. "I noticed a woman on the ferry. She was alone and continually glanced at our car, and the man in the car behind us was closely watching her."

"A tall blonde woman?" Phillip asked.

"Very pretty and above average in height. She was wearing what was obviously a black wig. If it was her, she led them to us without meaning to."

Phillip frowned. He didn't want to believe that Keri was a part of this, unintentional or not. They heard the thunderous roar of airborne engines again, powerful lights combing the island in circular patterns. As the choppers finally moved out over the water, the whirling drone growing fainter, Phillip thought of Keri and wondered where she was, what could he do? He quickly dismissed the thought that she might be in danger.

***

Chance Patton was waiting in the dingy inner city bar when Agent Voger arrived. They sat at a back table. Voger unscrewed the overhead light, said, "All we have to do now is wait."

"Pay back time," Patton said. "I just wish I was there. Bastards!"

Voger nodded. "After tonight Task Force Zero will slip back into the darkness from whence it came to await another opportunity to strike a blow for justice. But remember, my friend, nothing can ever be said about this operation."

"What about Phillip Lansing?"

Voger looked at his watch. "He's been terminated with the others."

"You think Keri learned anything before your men found her and returned her to the mainland?"

"No, she never got near Lansing." He took a gulp of his whiskey and put his hand on Patton's shoulder. "Look, you may as well know. We had to take her out."

Patton jerked his head around. "What do you mean, *out?*"

Voger looked at the ceiling. "We had to eliminate her. She's dead."

"Jesus!" Patton said, pushing back from the table. "You said she was safe!"

"Things change. She would have asked too many questions and we had no control over her."

Patton stood up. "Have you lost your mind? My God, Voger, you can't go around killing innocent people!"

He clinched his teeth. "Sit down and shut up. It was a judgment call, a necessary hit from my perspective."

"A stupid call!"

Voger reached up and caught him by the belt, pulled him into the chair. "I can't live with loose ends, and the task force is too important to America, to the world, to fret over the sacrifice of a potential troublemaker. We do what we have to do."

Patton removed his handkerchief and wiped his face. "All right, I can see that achieving our objective could be worth losing a couple of people in the process. I just wish Keri hadn't been one of them, sorry I lost control."

"Apology accepted." Voger ordered more drinks and the two were silent for a moment.

Patton thought back to the summer of ninety-nine when it all began. As if sensing his thoughts, Voger said, "If you hadn't told that reporter about your sister it wouldn't have made the news and you and I would have never met."

Drinks served, Patton said, "Yeah, getting a call from the FBI kind of shook us up, but when you said your mother had gone through a similar experience only a month before, it was as though an old friend had called."

The conversation was interrupted by the ringing of Voger's cell phone. It was Eric Turnell.

"What do you mean you can't find them?" Voger asked, rage in his voice.

"We covered the entire island. No sign of anyone, not even the car. The only thing we can figure is that a private ferry was waiting and took them somewhere else."

"Then find the damn thing!"

"We've been all over Puget Sound. Nothing, but we'll be back in the air at first light."

"Look, Turnell, there could be a couple of hundred of them getting together, maybe more. I want every facility large enough to accommodate that kind of crowd checked out. Keep concentrating on the islands."

"What if we run into questions from local authorities?"

"Tell them you're FBI working on a secret government operation and to keep their mouths shut."

"All right, in the morning we'll cover every island including Vancouver. We'll also take a look at charter boats and the private ferry lines. I'll call you every few hours with a report."

Voger thought a minute, breathing heavily. "I think I'd feel better about everything if I was personally on the scene. This is no time for screw-ups. Anyway, I've waited too long for this to remain a bystander. I'll be there by morning.

As Turnell replaced the receiver his gut tightened. He had never cared for Tony Voger, and his dislike was turning to hatred. He was glad he hadn't killed the old woman. She wouldn't remember him, even if Winslow's body was discovered some day.

Chapter 21

Mommy, Mommy...I'm so scared. Mommy please help me. Mommy! Kerianne? *Mommy, I'm coming.* The little blue-eyed girl with the blonde pony tail was running home, could hardly see in the heavy close-pressed darkness of the brooding night, soft wet grass under bare feet as she dashed across the fields toward the dim yellow light in the far distance, legs tired, tears on cheeks. Suddenly nothing but air...floating in space, then falling, falling, plunging into a grave so quiet. Utter stillness. And she heard her mother's gentle voice, reading again from Emerson's *Voluntaries*...

What his fault, or what his crime?
Or what ill planet crossed his prime?
Heart too soft and will too weak
To front the fate that crouches near...

Keri opened her eyes. Deep, cold darkness. A dream? She couldn't think, all a blur, a fog. Then it all came back in a rush: the FBI agent, the terror, the muffled sound of the gun, being shot. She shuddered, felt sharp pain, weakness enveloping her.

She pushed at the branches covering her and very slowly sat up, turning gently to lean against the rocky wall, her head pounding. She ran a hand carefully through her hair and over her face. Only a large knot on her forehead. More pain, her arm throbbing, a sticky substance covering her left hand, blood. She moved her other hand and felt the jacket sleeve wet and torn.

She remembered standing sideways to him. The bullet must have hit me in the arm, she thought. She touched her side and found a second hole in the windbreaker. *Oh God!* She unzipped the jacket and felt under the sweater--a long deep gash below her ribs, blood covering her stomach.

As her hand moved across her body, she discovered another tear in her clothing and understood why she was still alive, the moment vivid in her mind. She had brought her hand up just before he fired. The extended arm, and the billowing of the bulky sweater and jacket, gave her an enlarged profile. The bullet had passed through her arm just above the elbow, made a slash in her mid-section, and continued out through the sweater and jacket on the other side.

She felt the aching bump on her head again, pulled herself up and began the slow, painful climb out of the ravine.

***

Phillip, Alexandria, and the Matthews had gathered in a small parlor in the secret underground facility. Turning to Carlton, Phillip asked, "Why the FBI show of force? What do they know?"

"One of our people in the FBI office in New York called each one of us with a coded message. The agent had just learned about Task Force Zero, a rogue unit of the Bureau that wants us destroyed. He suggested we leave immediately. We had suspected we were being followed and our mission could soon be compromised, at least a part of it. And then those of us in government positions in other countries were alerted. We met with them earlier and they decided to return to their posts."

"How did your man in New York pick up on it?"

"He overheard two agents talking in what was supposed to be a soundproof office."

Phillip said, "If they know who you are, then fear is the reason they want you killed." Not getting a response he added, "But I can't believe that Director Brent would authorize such an operation, unless the president ordered it."

"Brent knew nothing about it," Alexandria said, "but he will soon. We don't have all the names, but now we know that Tony Voger heads up the Task Force."

A soft bell on the intercom signaled a voice transmission coming in. "Sorry to bother you Alexandria, but it appears we have someone in a prone position approximately two hundred meters from the primary entrance. The doors have remained closed, and I would not disturb you if the person did not seem to require assistance. Most desperately I would say. Functions of the body are most inefficient."

"Give me your graphic with full flesh-form pictorialization." Alexandria switched on the monitor, the screen blue.

"Just a moment, I will have to adjust." A rainbow array of colors danced in vertical ripples down the screen, then came together as a human form. It was a woman.

"My God, it's Keri," Phillip said as he stood and moved quickly to the monitor.

The voice said, "The body appears to be injured. What do you suggest I do?"

"Get to her fast," Carlton said, "and bring her to Station Four. We'll meet you there."

They were waiting when a man dressed in a white suit carried her in. "She has been shot," he said, "but the injuries are not sufficiently threatening to release her from the body." Keri was unconscious, head back, her breathing labored. Phillip was shocked at her appearance: jacket and hands covered in blood, face pale and scratched, a swelling on her forehead. She looked terrible and beautiful at the same time. He wanted to take her in his arms, hold her, tell her he wasn't angry she had followed him.

"Put her on the table," Alexandria said, "and Phillip, if you wouldn't mind stepping outside the room I'll see what Eve and I have to do."

"I'm not leaving her."

"Oh yes you are," Carlton said, taking him by the arm. "We'll wait in the hall. Ms. Winslow is in good hands."

***

Less than an hour later, Eve came out of the room to speak to Phillip and Carlton. "Keri is fully conscious and will be fine. She told us what happened. An FBI agent shot her and pushed her into a ravine, thought he'd killed her."

Carlton put his hand over his eyes and shook his head. "Probably on Voger's orders. He's a mad man, got to stop him."

Phillip stood, said, "Can I see her now?"

"Alexandria is still treating her wounds. She'll tell you when you can go in. Now I've got to find Robert Ames and brief him on the situation. I want him to have the information about Keri when he calls Washington."

Chapter 22

At the sound of the telephone Director Brent looked at the clock: 3:38 a.m. He switched on the light. Millie wasn't in bed. Couldn't sleep, he figured, probably in the kitchen getting a glass of milk. A phone in the middle of the night, her first thought would be about Jeff, Sharon and the baby in Houston, silently praying that everything was all right.

His concern wasn't about family; his gut said they were okay. The apprehension he felt now was that the case of the missing twelve was on a course that could only lead to a national dilemma of unimaginable proportions. He let the phone ring half a dozen times before answering it. "Brent here."

"Wallace, this is Robert Ames. We've got to talk."

"Mr. Attorney General, I-"

"Let's drop the titles, Wallace, and speak man to man. What I'm about to tell you may make you wish you were back on the ranch in Texas, but what you do after we hang up will make a crucial difference in preserving the integrity of our government."

Brent picked up a pad and pen from the nightstand and leaned back against the headboard. "I'm listening."

"There is a clandestine group of FBI agents called Task Force Zero. It was formed by Tony Voger. They have been secretly following and investigating certain government officials. To be specific, those of us who recently disappeared."

The director could see Ames in his mind, the square jaw, over-the-collar black hair and dark eyes. He had respected the man as a lawyer and admired his work as head of the Justice Department, but now there were suspicions. "If Voger was on to something, he had good reason. He's one of the top men in the Bureau."

"Then why did he keep Task Force Zero under cover?"

"Frankly I doubt that such a group exists. I think you're trying to throw us off from the real reason you people left town by trying to discredit Voger. Robert, why don't you and the others come back. I'll arrange an officially sanctioned meeting and you can tell your story. You may even want to reveal your real agenda."

Robert Ames forced a laugh. "I don't know what conclusions you've reached regarding the twelve of us, but if you can set your preconceived ideas aside, I'll give you some facts to work on."

The director was silent for a moment. "Go ahead."

"Wallace, we left Washington because Voger and his Task Force suspected that we supported and endorsed certain acts of fanaticism engaged in by individuals you might consider...I'll say inhuman for lack of a better term. We did not. We were found guilty by association. He believes that his mother died because of these people, and he vowed to eliminate all those linked to them in any way."

The director sighed. "Facts, Robert, facts. Identify the terrorist group and explain your connection."

Ames hesitated. "They are known as the Kawrs and they operate world wide with no allegiance to any particular country. You've never heard of them because they exist under the deepest cover possible. Their actions in the interest of self-serving research are rarely reported in the press. We know the Kawrs and have at times met with them in an effort to convince them that what they're doing is not beneficial to the cause. We feel that we've achieved a measure of success, and--"

"What kind of research?"

"Psychological and scientific. It's difficult to explain."

"You're skirting, dancing around. Damn it, be specific. Are you talking about brainwashing and experiments on human guinea pigs like our enemies did in the war?"

"To some extent, yes," Ames said, "but no one was killed."

"That's what you say. I don't know why Voger hasn't told me about such a group, but you as attorney general should certainly have kept the Bureau informed of any threat to national security."

"There was no such threat. The victims were isolated individuals, and a full report on the Kawrs and our connection with them will be forthcoming. But right now is a critical moment. An FBI agent in the Seattle field office, a man by the name of Eric Turnell, shot Keri Winslow last night, on Voger's orders we suspect. And FBI helicopters have been covering Puget Sound to find and destroy us."

Brent got off the bed and walked in a circle, phone in hand. "Are you sure they're our agents?"

"Absolutely."

"Are you in Seattle?"

"In the vicinity."

"You said Keri Winslow. Are you talking about the newswoman on Channel Eleven here in Washington?"

"Yes, she followed Phillip Lansing out here. He's the White House Correspondent for CBC Network. She was wounded but she'll be all right, and she has identified Turnell as the man who tried to kill her."

"I can't believe that."

"I do," Ames said.

The director shook his head. "How did he find her?"

"She said Randall Erickson, the station's news director, knew she was going out of town to gather information for a story, but he didn't know anything about Lansing or her destination. She thinks he may have called the FBI. If that's true, Erickson's part of the group. Winslow and Lansing are with us, but they won't be safe until every member of Task Force Zero has been apprehended. Now, Wallace, do I have your attention?"

"Yeah, but I'm wondering what you've left unsaid."

"You'll get the full story at the proper time and your every question will be answered. There won't be any doubt in your mind that we are loyal to America and everything this country stands for. In the meantime,

Wallace, can I rely on you to take immediate action? Remember, I'm still your boss and Voger and Task Force Zero must be stopped."

The director sat back on the bed. "All right, Mr. Attorney General. I may be crazy, but for some strange reason I trust you. I'll go to work on it right away."

"Call me when you've formulated your plan." Ames gave him the number where he could be reached and hung up.

Chapter 23

Brent walked into the kitchen and found Millie sitting at the table with several books including two dictionaries and a thesaurus. She was writing on a yellow pad. "Who was that on the phone?"

"Attorney General Ames with a story that's hard to believe."

"I've got one that's going to stretch your imagination, too. You can tell me about his later. Wallace, I think I've figured out the message the ambassador received."

"I don't have time for that now, got to call the president."

"You'd better take time. Pour yourself a glass of milk and sit down and listen." She waited as he followed instructions, then handed him the original paper. "Now follow me closely. Sigma has to be the name they're calling their group, and Sigma wary could mean *Sigma alert*, domestic, for those in the U.S. only. Let's use *uneasy* in place of awkward, *situation* instead of state, and *approaching* instead of drawing. Okay?" Her husband nodded. "Stay with me now. Chore power naught is--"

"Task Force Zero."

Millie looked up, surprised. "How did you know?"

"I'm a genius. But what's varlet eta-kin?"

She smiled. "Another word for varlet is rogue. Eta

is the seventh letter in the Greek alphabet. The seventh letter in ours is G and kin is men. Rogue G-men, Mr. Director." She noticed he didn't blink an eye. "But now for a couple of real kickers. Dicga is Old English for dog." She picked up a magnifying glass. "Look at the word awkward again and notice how the letter a is shaped, then drop down to the word oster." He did. "Notice anything?"

"The *o* in oster could be an *a*, which would spell aster."

"You catch on fast. And the translation of dicga asterkind is *Dog Star People,* and in case you didn't know, the Dog Star is Sirius. What this communication is saying is...*uneasy situation approaching as Task Force Zero of rogue FBI agents is moving to kill, erase, the people from Sirius.* Isn't this exciting?"

Brent looked at her with a blank stare.

She continued. "I just knew there was intelligent life out there, and I bet our missing people are in contact with them right now. And you're going to have the opportunity to prove it. God, honey, think what this will mean!"

Brent stood up and shook his head. "Millie, go back to bed. The lack of sleep has rattled your brain. You got part of it right but--"

"And the last line, suggest *immediate exit with synthesis in sealth islet,* means to get the hell out of here and come together again on an island off the coast of Seattle. Probably one of the San Juan Islands."

Brent's eyes widened. "How did you know about

Seattle?"

"The city was named after Chief Sealth, a Suquamish Indian chief. He was probably from Sirius too."

The director switched on the coffee and thought about Gillespie's report on Dome Light, and the massive reports of UFOs in fifty-four. *My God, I think we're all losing our minds!*

***

Special Agent Tony Voger finished packing and looked around his bedroom to see if he had everything. His gaze locked on the photograph of his mother, Ella Voger, and he immediately thought of Chance's sister, Ruth. Both had reported being abducted by strange people: hairless, very white faces with black eyes and wearing gray jumpsuits, but neither could remember details of the experience.

He wouldn't let Ella tell anyone about it. When Voger read about Ruth Patton, he called to suggest the two women undergo hypnosis to determine the truth. Both agreed, and with the aid of a hypnotherapist working secretly, Tony Voger heard a story from each of them that at the time he considered totally unbelievable. Later, the files were destroyed and Alan Sorenson, the hypnotist, was killed in an automobile accident.

Voger had listened to the tape of his mother's session with Sorenson so often he had committed it to memory. She had parked in the driveway of her home and was getting out of the car when she saw a light above her. *"Can't see anything but the light, hurts my eyes, no sound. Ohhh!"*

Sorenson told her to relax and tell him what was happening. *"I'm being lifted up, moving up a tube of light...I'm inside this cylinder rising slowly. Am I dying?"* Sorenson assured her she wasn't, and Ella Voger went on to say that she was being lifted into a room. *"White, very white room, a long table in the middle. It glistens in the light. There is a high ceiling... no, two stories. I see a winding staircase to the floor above...three people standing by a railing."*

They told her not to be afraid, that they were friends, and asked her to lie down on the table. As she did, she realized she didn't have any clothes on and began to cry. *"Where are my clothes? I don't have any clothes... what have they done with my clothes?* "Voger grimaced as he remembered his mother screaming from the needles that were inserted into her."*Oh dear Jesus, long needles everywhere in me... no blood... my whole body lit up like a light inside. "*

And then she described a whining sound and feeling electric currents. *"It doesn't hurt, but the voltage is shaking me and light inside of me is flashing in different colors."* There was a silence on the tape and after a moment she began to speak again. *"I have my clothes on. They say they are my friends and are telling me that I can get up and walk around. Oh...dizzy. Okay now. One of them is going up the staircase now and I feel I am to follow him. Another one is behind me. He says not to be afraid. I'm gliding to the second floor, going into a library ... very many books... and people on the wall. "*

When Sorenson asked what she meant by people on the wall, she said, *"Color sketches, portraits I guess, lots of them. People who look like us. Oh, I see someone I recognize. It's that famous Washington attorney, Robert Ames.* Pause. *I didn't know that. "*

"Know what?" Sorenson asked.

"Mr. Ames only appears to be human. He isn't. The person with me said Mr. Ames is one of them, from their world, and there are many more from their world who will soon be in our higher government."

Ruth Patton also reported seeing Robert Ames' likeness in a gallery on a "stark white wall." Voger was stunned, couldn't understand about Ames or the strange creatures. He had heard about the continuous UFO investigations from other intelligence agencies and the deep cover projects authorized in the highest levels of government, but he had never believed there were other intelligent life-forms in this universe.

Ella Voger died of a heart condition the following year, followed shortly with Ruth taking an overdose of pills in what was thought to be a suicide. Agent Voger immediately began a personal and top secret examination of reports from the Center for UFO Studies, the Defense Intelligence Agency, and the CIA. Satisfied he wasn't dealing in fantasy or fiction, he organized Task Force Zero to track down, root out and destroy everyone suspected of being an alien. In his mind, they were all murderers.

Voger searched the personnel files in the Bureau's master computer looking for agents whose records showed signs of over-zealousness. He focused particularly on agents who had felt the Bureau's wrath after September 11, 2001. He also looked for those who had filed grievances against their superiors or had been disciplined for disobeying orders. Every known malcontent was put on the list, their profiles carefully screened, with more than a third rejected because of recent psychological testing 'with favorable results' noted.

Once the final roster was ready, Voger met secretly with each agent in cautious in-depth interrogation. No one was told about Task Force Zero and the objectives of the unit until Voger was certain the agent met all the qualifications: total loyalty to Voger, a passion for deep-cover operations outside the jurisdiction of the Bureau, a rabid personality that would follow any order in the name of cause.

Voger also set up what he called the 'watcher system'. Within each field office he placed an informer, unknown to the other agents, who would report to Voger of any weakness in the ranks. He made it clear that if he ever received such a report, the agent in question would be removed from the Task Force, and the men knew what this implied. Intimidation seemed to add to the intrigue, and the group quickly developed a camaraderie and a dedication to Voger's agenda while remaining invisible to the main FBI organization and the intelligence community.

To gather evidence and verify the claims of Ella and Ruth, Robert Ames had been followed wherever he went. Video surveillance began when he was named attorney general. When Ames' closest friends in government were finally identified, Voger assigned a member of Task Force Zero to eliminate each one. Then they suddenly disappeared. One of his men thought he had caught Senator Obrey leaving his home. Mistaken identity. Voger surmised that the aliens had somehow been tipped off and had gone underground to meet with their kind from other countries. But they would not get away,

***

Phillip and Carlton sat in chairs just outside the door to Station Four. Carlton leaned back, said, "Phillip, do you recall the reports of German doctors experimenting on men and women in the concentration camps?" He nodded. "The victims were frozen, sterilized, shot with poison bullets to test the effects, given injections of typhus, and literally skinned alive." Phillip closed his eyes to block out the horror. "And do you recall the stories revealing how U.S. military intelligence deliberately exposed our soldiers to radiation, chemicals and hallucinatory drugs to test the effect on the mind and physical system?"

"Yes, I know about that," Phillip said, "but it wasn't only the military. University scientists under orders from our government also injected hospital patients with uranium and plutonium without their knowledge. It was done to test the effect of atomic radiation on their bodies."

"Well, we have a less cruel but in some ways a similar state of consciousness existing in our world. We call those with it the Kawrs. They are originally from a far-distant galaxy and are not considered malevolent. But their total fascination is on the physical body. They simply don't understand how or why energy-as-form can suffer and die."

Phillip looked at his friend. "So what are you saying?"

"I'm saying that Tony Voger's mother was subjected to various tests by a group of Kawrs. She later died of a pre-existing heart condition, but Voger blames...well, what he calls aliens, for her death. That's why he formed Task Force Zero, to eliminate us."

"How did Voger know about you and the others?"

"Our man in the FBI called here with additional information about Task Force Zero. He had planted our recording devices in every suspected agent's office and car and soon put more of the pieces together. He learned that under hypnosis Mrs. Voger remembered seeing what you would call a photograph of Robert Ames, and she heard one of the Kawrs say he was part of their group. There was another woman, a Ruth Patton, who corroborated the story while in a trance."

Phillip asked, "Why did he say that Ames was a Kawr?"

"He really didn't. We frequently visit the various planes of existence, and the Kawrs look to us as their Elders. To say that we are associated with them is simply a point of pride. We are from the same world, but far from the same dimensional frequency. Anyway, Voger set up his covert operation and began following Ames. As we all moved into government positions and stayed close, we became suspects too."

"But--"

Phillip's response was interrupted by a smiling

Alexandria at the door.

Chapter 24

As Phillip entered the large white room to see Keri, he experienced another of what seemed to be the unending shocks that had jarred him since arriving in Seattle. She was sitting on a couch drinking liquid from a cup, obviously freshly bathed, hair combed, the hint of makeup on her face obscuring the scratches. A small silver patch was on her forehead, a silver bandage around her arm. She was wearing a sleeveless white robe.

"God, Keri, you look wonderful! How do you feel?"

She smiled softly and looked down at the floor. "You aren't mad at me?"

He walked over and knelt down beside her. "Not at all. I'm just glad you're all right. You sure were a mess when you were brought in. Eve Matthews gave us the details. You're lucky to be alive."

She put her hand on his. "Alexandria doctored the wounds, then put something she called an energy wrap on my arm and around me. She said the lacerations would soon be healed. And look at my head. There's hardly any swelling. I don't understand."

He moved up and sat on the couch beside her, his arm around her shoulders. "I'll explain later. There's so much we have to talk about." Careful to avoid the injured arm, he leaned over and kissed her gently. She turned her body to his, put both arms around him and held him close. He felt her tears falling on his cheek, knew that it was more than the physical body that needed healing. She had been through an emotional nightmare, and only time and loving care would be the mending agent for that inner wound.

He lifted her chin and she opened her lips. He kissed her again, pressing eagerly, the salt of her tears in his mouth adding to the fervor of the moment, their bodies electric, seeking more.

The embrace was broken at the sound of Alexandria entering the room. "Sorry to intrude. Keri, you'll need to change. We'll be traveling in the morning. You're taller than I am but we have the same body build. I think these will do nicely. Here's a small purse containing everything from your pockets." She placed the purse and clothing on the table. "We disposed of your other things the psychic energy was very heavy."

Phillip noticed the expression on Keri's face. Wanting to avoid questions at this time, he said, "What I think she needs most is a little sleep, and I could use a few winks myself."

"I'm sorry," Alexandria said, "I didn't think of that. We never sleep and it slipped my mind that you people still need that out-of-body experience."

They reach no term, they never sleep,
In equal strength through space abide.

"Keri, are you all right?" Phillip asked.

She blinked her eyes. "Oh, yes...1 was just remembering part of a poem my mother used to read to me." She stood and looked into Alexandria's eyes "Who are you?"

"Phillip can tell you later. I'll take you to your room so you can rest."

Keri stepped back. "No, I want *you* to tell me now."

Phillip pulled a chair over to the couch. "Sit down Alexandria, and we'll make this a threesome. You can start, then I'll repeat what you told me earlier. It will be a good practice for remembering when I begin the book."

"What book?" Keri asked as she sat back on the couch.

"The one you and I are going to write together. Now, Alexandria, let's begin with the opening statement you made to me in the hotel."

She settled in the chair, reached over and touched Keri's hand. Speaking slowly and softly, she said, "Keri, I am not of this world. Neither are the others who are with me. We are interdimensional beings, people from a non-physical universe on a coordinate corresponding to the star you call Sirius."

Keri stared at her with an open mouth. Finally she said, "You've got to be kidding."

"She's not," Phillip said. "They are the Sigma group on a major expedition to earth. While there have been many visitations from their world during our history as a planet, there have only been a few massive infiltrations. This is number eighteen. Sigma is the eighteenth letter in the Greek alphabet, and millions of them are here now."

"We arrived in nineteen fifty-four," Alexandria said, "and took on the bodies of children. We lived lives in physical form to become fully synchronized with the collective consciousness of your world. This immersion into the energy of the mass mind was necessary to understand your basic thoughts and feelings, but in doing so we temporarily lost our power of telepathic communications among ourselves and the ability to instantly read your minds, which would have been quite normal otherwise. As was planned, several of us rose to high positions of government, not only in this country but abroad."

Keri continued to appear stunned. "You look like us?"

"What you are seeing as a physical body," Alexandria said, "is what I am projecting with my mind."

"But I can feel your touch."

"Of course. I brought the body into full materialization, and I can make it disappear through the same process. While in the flesh, however, we can let ourselves age. I stopped the aging process at thirty. The others waited until later to slow it down."

"What do you really look like?"

"Those in our world function as a body of sculptured light with little physical characteristics."

Keri shook her head. "Does your world mean another planet?"

"Not necessarily. As I said, we are

interdimensionals, a better word than extraterrestrials. There are two universes, Keri, the visible, which is finite, and the infinite invisible with multiple dimensions of reality, the many mansions." She paused. "I say *invisible*, yet we can project any image into an etheric form of visibility, with color I might add. We live in beauty."

"You're from what we call heaven?"

Alexandria stood, took a measured step. "The immediate afterlife realm is one level. We live beyond that in a higher frequency, a world of energies that ascends to the Absolute, the highest cosmic realm of pure consciousness. While we have not yet evolved to that level, we do have the full realization that we are divine expressions of our Creator."

"Are you an angel?"

Alexandria smiled. "We have been called angels, particularly in biblical times."

Keri could feel her investigative instincts kicking in. "Angels have been referred to as messengers of God. Are you?"

Alexandria turned to face her. "Every reference to angels in the Bible and other scriptural works speaks of us. And yes, we have been in communication with the people of Earth for aeons." She noticed Phillip pull a small notebook from his pocket and begin to write. She continued. "Before the advent of the major religions, we placed monoliths in ancient lands, on the site of what is now the Kailasa Temple at Ellora in the Himalayas, the desert where the Great Pyramid was eventually built, and on the grounds where cities known as Rome, Jerusalem, and Mecca would be established,"

"Monoliths with messages?" Keri asked.

"Yes, carved on the stones, first in cuneiforms then hieroglyphics, later in the appropriate ancient language. Although in capsule form, a minimum of words, the key points protracted in today's English would be that God Is, that each individual is a complete expression of the Infinite Is, with neither wrath nor judgment from God, only love. Unfortunately, the shadows of the collective mind blocked out the truth, and man created his own gods in the image of his false self."

As Alexandria sat down, Keri stood and began to pace, wishing the room had some color in it. The omnipresent white seemed so glaring. She shook her head, focused on her thoughts. "This country was founded by Christians. Did your people have a role in that?"

Alexandria shifted in her chair. "We do not favor any particular religion as all are divisive in one way or another. You should remember that your founding fathers were, for the most part, Deists. Thomas Jefferson and Benjamin Franklin, for example, believed in God but not in the Christian view. To them, God was the *natural* order of the universe rather than supernatural. This was the position of Thomas Paine, too. Their God would not have helped Joshua kill his enemies by delaying the setting of the sun. No, divine activity was based on perfect order, spiritual law, unconditional love for all."

Phillip stopped writing for a moment. "I seem to recall a stranger mysteriously appearing during the debate over the Declaration of Independence and--"

Alexandria interrupted. "He was one of us. Peter Lang by name. His sudden appearance among the debaters was shocking, and he spoke only seven words before vanishing. *God has given America to be free*. At that moment wild enthusiasm burst forth and the Declaration of Independence was signed." She smiled. "We come where we are needed."

Keri settled back on the couch with Phillip, glanced at Alexandria. "Was Jesus an interdimensional?"

"Yes. He came from a coordinate near Venus, and that identification remained. This is why he was referred to as the *bright morning star*, Venus, in Revelation. I should add that the symbol of the fish, which you see on many automobiles today as a Christ symbol, is directly related to Venus. The custom of eating fish on Friday was because *Friday* was the Scandinavian word for Venus." She paused. "Jesus came to Earth not to be a blood sacrifice to wash away sins. He came to teach the law of love, to open hearts to truth, and help you understand your oneness with God. Others from our world have come with the same mission."

There was silence in the room. Finally Keri asked, "How did you come to Earth?"

"We can move into your three-dimensional sphere by lowering our vibration in consciousness to match your frequency world."

"Then *you* are not a part of the UFO folklore."

"They *are* the UFOs," Phillip said. "Every time they break through the veil, a cosmic vibration of immense energy is set off, an explosive force in the web of collective consciousness that separates the two worlds. This registers in the mind-aggregate of those on earth as an unidentified phenomena. Some see it visually, others only feel it as a psychic shock."

"And that doesn't happen during a death-and-return experience," Alexandria said, "because the silver cord is not broken. And neither is there a flare and luminous trail in the mind-web when someone who has recently passed on slips back through the veil for momentary duty, usually to comfort a loved one. They simply don't have our reservoir of energy."

"But people have seen spaceships."

"Those are materialized holographic projections," Phillip said. "One particular group from the world beyond continues to use virtual images of spacecraft when they pass through the vortex into this world." He knocked on the wall. "And the ships are as solid as this is."

Alexandria smiled. "We used flying objects originally to get the attention of the early humans, and those images have remained in the collective psyche. The writers of the Old Testament thought we were gods."

Speak it firmly, these are gods,
All are ghosts beside.

Keri listened to the line playing in her mind, then to Alexandria's voice. "To the early people, some theatrics were often necessary. Read the beginning passages in the book of Ezekiel. Phillip can give you other 22 examples." She stood up. "I'll take you to your rooms now."

"One more question," Keri said. "Who else knows the truth about you, who you really are?"

Alexandria thought for a moment. "There are a few men and women on the planet today who believe in the *possibility* of a race of beings such as ours, but they don't know for sure. As far as UFO investigators, they are following the reports of those from a lower dimension who use materialized holograms. They simple cannot travel instantaneously as our group can. Now, as far as people who have experienced our presence, we have worked closely with several for thousands of years." She nodded with a smile. "I had a *close encounter* with a man in the 1500s, and--"

Phillip didn't look up from his notebook. "His name."

"Giordana Bruno. I helped him expand on the Copernican theory of the universe. He was originally a Dominican friar but renounced his monastic order because he didn't believe the miracle of the Eucharist. In his new role as a metaphysician, he was open to truth, and through new revelations he was able to see the universe as infinite and understand there were innumerable worlds inhabited by living beings with a greater God within each soul." She sighed. "For his blasphemy against the Pope and his conception of the universe, he was turned over to the Inquisition and was burned at the stake on February 17, 1600."

She walked toward the door. "More discussion later. Keri, I want you to rest now, and Phillip, there is a computer and printer in your room. Start compiling your notes. I'll come by for both of you later. We're meeting the others in the living room at five in the morning."

Chapter 25

They took an elevator down to the third level, reaching Phillip's room first. He kissed Keri and said, "Sleep well, we'll talk later." She touched his cheek and nodded.

As Alexandria opened Keri's door further down the hall, Keri asked, "Can't I stay with Phillip? I really don't want to be alone."

"Are you lovers?"

"Well, I...I *want* us to be. I love him very much."

Alexandria smiled. "I believe the feeling between you is mutual, but love making is off limits for now."

"I didn't mean--"

"Intercourse would be a highly beneficial therapy for you both, but you'll have to wait." She paused. "Keri, I could have healed you completely, literally in a matter of seconds, but that would have frightened you, affected you mentally and emotionally. When something of a dramatic and highly beneficial nature suddenly happens to a human, particularly in an instantaneous healing, fear of the unknown can negate the return to wholeness. A this-can't-be-true apprehension sets in which rejects the restoration. That's why humans do not have more of what you would call spontaneous manifestations."

"I think I understand."

"So I used the energy wraps. Heavy passion would

interfere with the pulsations, and I don't want anything to delay the healing process. You'll be as good as new by this time tomorrow, and you'll be free to follow your heart."

Keri wanted to tell her that making love had not entered her mind, but she would be lying. "Do you do it over there?" Keri immediately regretted asking the question.

Alexandria glanced up in a moment of thought. "Well, not as you do here. Our bodies are pillars of light. And our love for each light, for one another, is complete. However, we may experience a twin-flame relationship where the light pulsations are on a near-identical energy tone. The vibrations are so similar we can bond in what you might call orgasmic ecstasy. We simply merge, interfuse to where we become one light."

"Do you call it love making?"

"We refer to it as *nweering*." She spelled the word. "The closest way to describe it is a near-loss of consciousness in rapture."

"I haven't experienced anything like *that* before."

"You will," Alexandria said. "Perhaps you have found your energy equivalent in Phillip."

Keri smiled without commenting. As the smile faded she said, "I'll be glad when this is all over."

Alexandria said, "I know there is still some underlying fear concerning the hours and days ahead, but Robert Ames has called the FBI Director, and the dissolution of Task Force Zero should be underway shortly."

"You said earlier we'd all be traveling soon. Where are we going?"

"You and Phillip will be hidden on the mainland until you can make it back to Washington."

"Why can't we stay here until--"

"I'm sorry, no. We can't expose this facility to outsiders. Director Brent and one of our people in the FBI will meet you at a private residence in Bellevue."

"What about you and the others?"

"They will return to our world; the exposure has jeopardized their work. Now that Voger has identified the twelve they are too vulnerable, and the questions would be interminable. I will stay on the island with my staff to oversee the large contingent of our people who will remain on earth to complete the mission."

Keri asked, "Are you saying that *you* are in charge of Sigma? I thought Carlton was."

Alexandria smiled. "He is my second in command. I planned the entire operation and have lived here with my staff since entering your world in nineteen fifty-four. Someone else will be taking his place, and please don't ask who that is."

"One more question. Why is the Sigma group on earth at this time?"

There was a look of joy in Alexandria's black eyes. "To put it in the most basic of terms, dear Keri, we have come to hasten the end of your world."

Chapter 26

"Mr. Director, do you know what time it is?"

"Yes, I do. Now put the call through."

The President answered on the first ring. "Yes?"

"Sir, I apologize for disturbing your sleep. This is Director Brent and we need to get together as quickly as possible."

"Couldn't sleep, was reading. I take it you've heard something about the missing people."

"I've been on the phone with Attorney General Ames. He told me a pretty wild story, said FBI agents in Seattle are trying to kill him and the others. The agents are part of a group called Task Force Zero formed by Tony Voger. I'll give you a full report in person."

"And you believe him?"

"Mr. President, I don't know what I believe." He glanced out the window at the street light, thought about Millie's translation pointing to visitors from outer space, decided against mentioning it. "However, my gut tells me that there may be some truth to what the attorney general said. One of the network people, White House correspondent Phillip Lansing, is with them. Also a TV woman from one of the stations here, Keri Winslow. She reported that an agent shot her and she has identified him. It's a real can of worms."

"My chief of staff, Bob Evans, may be responsible for stirring things up. He confessed to me last evening that he called the Winslow woman and told her the story was true, that the twelve had suddenly disappeared without a trace. He's from Baltimore and was impressed with her investigative work when she was a TV reporter there. He felt she and her cohorts could get to the bottom of it faster than the FBI, that they could dig where you couldn't."

"He might be right," Brent said. "People tip the media more than they do the authorities. Maybe Evans thought Winslow could turn up another deep throat, but she was in trouble from the start. Someone at Channel Eleven called Voger and his people were watching for her in Seattle. We're going over to the station this morning, but I want to meet with you first."

"Are you coming alone?"

Brent looked at his notepad. "No sir, I've called Assistant Director Gillespie and Agent Benton Fowler who oversees criminal investigations. I also asked Assistant Attorney General Wright to be there. I told them I'd call them back as soon as I could arrange an appointment with you."

"We'll meet in the Oval Office in an hour."

"Thank you, Mr. President."

***

Phillip was typing on the computer in his room. He stopped, yawned, and went back to page one to see if what he had written made any sense. He had begun with a detailed outline of what he titled 'Sigma Rising,' recalling Alexandria had said Sigma represented a major opportunity to rise up and confront the ignorance and misunderstanding that was holding humanity in bondage. He then added some preliminary notes:

She called herself Alexandria Day, a beautiful woman, about thirty in appearance but in truth ageless, beyond time. Not of this world she had said, an entity from another universe--non-physical, pure energy, celestial.

Her world is a galactic cluster on a coordinate parallel to the physical counterpart of Sirius in the constellation Canis Major. She lives in an imaged crystal city surrounded by the magnificent splendor of what we might call nature in all its glory. Even the flowers sing, she said, in tribute to their creator.

She says they are interdimensional beings living on a higher frequency, and they enter our world by lowering their energy vibrations from sattvic to tamasic (Sanskrit), or fine to gross. This causes a shock wave in the collective consciousness of humanity and registers as an unexplained phenomenon. When I asked about the sightings on radar, she said, "Weather changes are picked up on radar. Our breakthrough in the mind-web causes a much more severe disturbance."

The Kawrs, on the other hand, come from a plane corresponding to the constellation Reticulum. They move into earth atmosphere at a vortex in cislunar space in a process similar to what physicists call "warping"--a literal shrinking of space. They create a virtual image (hologram) of a spaceship and then materialize it. If any of the materials of the ship are ever found, they will not match anything known to our science.

Alexandria explained their use of holographic projections of "ships in the sky" during the early days on this planet, saying that a subtle form of authority and control had to be provided in order to place the people in a "reverent state of mind."

The experiments on earth people by the Kawrs were explained. When taken "up" to a mother ship or space craft they are entering a materialized hologram. She said rather than projecting a desired physical appearance, the Kawrs materialize their light bodies for earth-plane activity. The result is a strange appearance with exaggerated features.

Alexandria said that millions of her fellow beings are on earth to help humanity break through the illusion of this world and enter into the reality that has been here all the time. Appearing as normal human beings, they have taken their places in all walks of life and in most every type of business and profession. While they have truly supernatural powers, they do not usually draw attention to themselves and are careful to protect their identities.

Their first visit was two million years ago to bring humans into a state of conscious self-awareness. They were a part of our prehistory, she said. They returned again in 9045 B. C. to accelerate our awakening and contribute to the rapid development of our civilization.

She talked about a group, the Cheus, from a plane corresponding to the planet Neptune who moved through the veil to earth beginning in 5400 B. C. to bring us spiritual truths and the esoteric tradition of philosophy. She said, "They did not create religions, for such a system is unknown in the non-physical universe. There is only the adoration of the one creator who resides in the heart of each individual."

Another group, from the non-physical counterpart to the Pleiades, follows one of the Great Rays and comes through the etheric body of Mercury. They also enter earth in cislunar space and materialize virtual images. Their work is primarily devoted to seeding the race mind with ideas to protect the environment, warn of earth changes, and help us get more in tune with the natural process of nature. They are known as the Neis.

The Sigma group, known as the Asters, came into the earth frequency again in 1954. "Otherwise, "she said, "your world would have experienced a nuclear war in the 1960s. Through our energy we changed the vibration of the planet, but the physically trapped respond in many different ways. The energy of peaceful relations was reinterpreted in the minds of some humans as a discontent with traditions, and the discarding of old restraints inspired the counter-culture movement. And because the collective mind is so heavily weighted in favor of explosive antagonism, ethnic feuds, repressed religious rivalries, and power struggles among nations rose to the surface."

Later Alexandria said, "The world as you know it will end, but not through mass destruction. We are here to help you achieve that final hour in another way." When I asked her to explain this, she said, "The world seen through human physical eyes is an illusion created by the collective mind of humanity and is filled with fear and death. Fear and death are not real, therefore this world is not real. When the thoughts of mind that created this world are changed, your experience of this world will change as truth emerges from the shadows. The rent in the veil between the two universes will then be complete, and there will be a coming and going at will. There will be no birth or death, which were not an original part of the natural process. There will be only the adventure of continuous joyful life."

Phillip looked around as the door opened. "I thought you were asleep."

Keri walked over and sat on the bed. She was still wearing her white robe. "I tried, but my nerves are a little on edge."

"I understand. Why don't you stretch out in here and I'll shut this thing down for awhile. We've got a few hours before Alexandria comes by."

"Please continue with your writing. I didn't mean to bother you. I just wanted some company. I'm also a bit concerned about something Alexandria said." She repeated her end-of-the-world statement.

Phillip turned to the computer and read the part about the illusory world. "It's not real, Keri, it's part of the mass dream, and the dream world will disappear when the majority of humankind awakens to reality."

"What reality?"

"The truth that we're just like Alexandria and the others: expressions of God, of Divine Love, created in a state of perfection, and we will, in time, return to that completeness."

She shook her head, confused. "Maybe so, but all I want to think about right now is being with you."

He moved to the side of the bed. "Keri, when this is all over we're going to be practically inseparable."

She smiled. "What does that mean?"

He touched her face. "It means I love you." He took her in his arms and kissed her tenderly, held her close.

"I've thought a lot about us since I got on that plane to follow you out here, and it's funny...when I was in the car with that FBI agent...just a few minutes before... anyway, all I could think about was you, how much I loved you, not wanting you to be angry with me."

He looked into her eyes. "I've felt deeply about you since almost the beginning of our relationship. When you were brought in here, the thought you could have been killed and I'd never see you again made me understand even more how much you mean to me."

"What if we had both stayed in Washington and not gotten caught up in all this drama and intrigue? Would we feel the way we do now?"

"What happened here compressed the time element."

She put her hand on his shoulder. "I believe it was Gibran who said *let there be spaces in your togetherness*. I agree, but right now I'm not interested in any distance between us."

He smiled "In case you wondered, I've been physically attracted to you since our first encounter. I wanted to see where the relationship was going before I made any moves. You probably felt the same way."

"Maybe, but what I think is that we were too caught up in trying to figure out what makes President Underwood tick and who's in and out in official Washington. We let busy-ness get in the way." She leaned over and touched his lips with hers. "Phillip, let's get married."

"I was about to ask you. And we will, just as soon as we can." He kissed her eyes and ear, breathing hard as his hand moved down to the small of her back and pulled her body firmly against his.

She felt his arousal and smiled. "Just as soon as we can, but we'll let the wounds heal first. Alexandria said it would only take another day, and for me not to engage in any passionate activity until then."

He laughed as he pulled her back on the bed, his arm around her shoulder. "Well at least this is a first," he said. "We've never been in bed together before."

Within minutes both were sound asleep.

Chapter 27

The president was wearing a sweater and slacks when the three men entered the Oval Office. He shook hands with Director Brent, Assistant Attorney General Wright, and Agent Fowler. "I thought you said Assistant Director Gillespie was coming."

"He'll be joining us later, Mr. President. He's at the Bureau now, working with our top computer boys, agents we think we can trust, trying to find anything on Task Force Zero. Hopefully he'll be bringing us some good news."

The president slowly nodded, was silent for a moment, then said with a smile, "Gentlemen, pour yourselves a cup of coffee. I've arranged for some breakfast a bit later. Now, Wallace, let's hear what you have."

Director Brent gave him a detailed report of his conversation with Attorney General Ames and answered the president's questions as best he could. Again he decided not to mention Millie's interpretation of the coded message. "And I learned just before coming here that Tony Voger took one of our jets without authorization. We didn't want him to know we're on to him, so we didn't try to make radio contact and order his return."

Fowler said, "I've sensed for some time that Voger was over-stressed, but I think he's gone off the deep end."

Brent took a sip of coffee. "I'd call the Seattle field office and have the plane met, but frankly, I don't know who to trust."

Assistant Attorney General Wright said, "Since it appears the renegades are confined to the Bureau and the Seattle area, I suggest we call in the military there for assistance."

Brent gave him a long look. "I don't like that idea. I'd rather wash our own dirty laundry, keep this thing as quiet as possible."

There was a knock on the door. Assistant Director Gillespie was shown in, a large smile on his face. "Good morning, Mr. President." He turned to Director Brent and handed him a manila folder. "We broke the code. The list of agents belonging to Task Force Zero is in there. There are eighty-three in all, twenty here in Washington, half a dozen in New York. The rest are scattered across the country."

"How many in the Pacific Northwest?" the president asked.

"Fourteen. They are operating essentially as a swat team assembled on a directive with the code of *minutemen*. The other agents consider it a no questions asked, top secret priority mission initiated by the director."

"Are they in for a surprise," Brent said, "and better odds than I thought." Glancing toward the president, he asked, "May I use your phone?"

The director called the heads of the FBI field

offices in Washington and Oregon and briefed each one on the situation. The first call to Seattle included information on Voger's plane and instructions to hold him and the pilot at the airport. He gave the names of the agents in Task Force Zero and said photo faxes would be on the wire soon. He instructed his men to break into airborne and mobile land teams and to work the area in square mile grids.

During his final call he looked at his watch. "It's six-thirty here. Call the others back and tell them I'm taking a Bureau jet out of here and should be at the Seattle-Tacoma airport around ten your time. I want a field supervisor's meeting in the security officer's office at the airport when I arrive. Set that up and make sure we're patched into every unit on the scene."

Brent hung up and reached into his pocket for another number and called Robert Ames. He didn't hear the ring signal and was about to redial when Ames answered. "Robert, I'm in the president's office now and have contacted all the Northwest field offices. Gillespie found their names in the computer. My agents will be traveling by chopper and car to locate and apprehend each member of Task Force Zero. And I'll be on my way out there as soon as I can finish up a few more details here. My advice to you is to stay hidden until I give you the all clear, then we'll bring you all back to Washington."

Ames didn't respond immediately. "You'll find Keri Winslow and Phillip Lansing in a private home in Bellevue, across Lake Washington from Seattle." He gave him the address. "The home is unoccupied at the moment; it belongs to a friend. Keri and Phillip will be waiting for you."

"Will you and the others be there too?"

"Some of us will meet you there. And Wallace, another close friend of mine is one of your agents in New York, David Gasparri."

"I know him, a good man. He's come up fast."

"He's a tactical genius and I think he can be of great help in this situation. He might even be the ideal candidate to replace Voger. He's earned it, and he's the one who uncovered Voger's plan. The reason you weren't notified was because he didn't know who to trust in the Bureau."

Brent rolled his eyes. "I know the feeling."

"I've been on the phone with David and told him to take the DC shuttle and join you in your efforts to track down Voger. He'll be waiting at your office. Good luck, Wallace. Now I have someone here who wants to speak to the president. Put him on. "

He passed the phone over. "Hello Robert. Oh, good morning... it's been awhile." The president listened. The only other words he spoke for nearly two minutes were, "I understand." As he replaced the receiver, Brent noticed a look of melancholy on his face.

"Sir, are you all right?"

"Yes, I'm fine." He looked at the director. "Are we about through here? I have some work to do."

Brent turned to Agent Fowler. "Benton, get a team

together in each city and find every member of Task Force Zero on that list. I want them brought here. No media leaks."

"Yes sir."

"And I'll brief Justice," said Wright. "I'll say that arrests are imminent, that you'll have sufficient evidence to present for prosecution."

Brent nodded, returned his attention to Fowler. "I want agents to find Randall Erickson, at that television station or his home. Determine if he called Voger with information about Winslow and Lansing, and if not who did. We may have a Zero man or woman over there, and I want the person brought in for questioning. "

"I'll take care of it."

"All right, Mr. President, we'll get out of your hair and I'll call you as soon as we have Voger and his task force in custody."

"Fine." The president showed the men to the door, shook their hands, and after a few minutes went to his private quarters. His wife Julia was looking out the window when he came in. He said, "They're not coming back."

She didn't turn around. "I know. They're going home."

"Well, I guess I'd better start thinking about what to say to the press when Director Brent comes back without them. Any ideas?"

"Not right now," the first lady said, her voice barely above a whisper.

**

Alexandria opened the door to Phillip's room. Seeing the two in deep sleep she moved past the bed to the computer and began typing as fast as the machine could register the words. Hardly a sound was made as her fingers flew across the keys. At four twenty-five a.m. she pushed the print button and turned to look at the man and woman holding each other.

In a soft voice she said, "Dear ones, it is time to wake up."

Phillip opened his eyes. He stretched and felt Keri move in closer, her head on his shoulder. "Keri, you have to dress," Alexandria said. "We will be leaving the island before dawn."

Keri sat up and rubbed her eyes. "Nothing happened. I just wanted to be with Phillip."

Alexandria sat on the edge of the bed. "You'll have your personal lives back in order soon, but the next few hours are of critical importance."

Phillip studied her closely, "Are you taking us off the island?"

"I've arranged for a boat to be at the dock. Nine of us will be leaving together. We'll take it across to the mainland where cars will be waiting for us and we'll drive you to a residence in Bellevue. Your clothes from the hotel are there. One of my people checked you out and returned Keri's rental car. We'll wait in Bellevue for Director Brent."

She motioned toward the computer. "Phillip, I've given you more details for the book. The pages are being printed now along with your input. Put them in your case. It is vitally important that the people of the world be prepared for what is to come."

Phillip nodded. "Thanks. I still had a lot of questions."

She looked at Keri. "Go change clothes and meet us back here. Most of the others have already moved beyond the veil, but Carlton and Eve Matthews, Robert and Paula Ames, and Merriam Livingston-Vance and her husband George will stay with us until we're sure you're out of harm's way. Hurry now."

As Keri left the room, Phillip said, "I would have thought that with your powers, you people could zap the bad guys, you know, immobilize them somehow so you wouldn't have to worry about us."

"There is possible danger ahead for you and Keri, but we do not interfere with free will. What others may do, they will do of choice from their state of mind. We will not change that. Our role will be to protect you without violating universal laws."

"But what about you? You would certainly defend yourself if someone was about to take your life."

"I would not defend through aggression, if that is what you mean. Remember, Phillip, I cannot die, and neither can you. Yes, it is possible that you and Keri could lose your bodies, and this is why we want to offer you our protection. But you cannot lose your lives." She motioned to the door. "It's time, Phillip. We'll stop by Keri's room. She may be having difficulty fitting into my things."

He gathered the papers from the printer and put

them in his briefcase. As they stepped into the hall Keri was walking toward them. She was dressed in a pale blue ruffled shirt, dark blue skirt and loafers. A cream-colored velvet peacoat was on her shoulders. "Neat clothes, Alexandria. Where do you shop?"

Alexandria pointed to above her head. "In my mind."

Keri noticed she was wearing a classic winter-white sheath. She liked Alexandria's creations. Simple but sophisticated.

***

It was five forty-five a.m. when Tony Voger's plane touched down at the Yakima airport. A helicopter with Turnell on board was waiting to take him to Olympic National Park northwest of Seattle where other agents were waiting.

Chapter 28

They took the elevator to the first floor and entered the large living room where the group was waiting. Alexandria introduced Keri to Robert and Paula Ames, Merriam and George Vance. Keri was still finding it difficult to believe they weren't regular down to earth humans. She thought about the people from her childhood, those she had worked with in television, and the men and women living in her apartment building. She wondered if any were interdimensionals.

After warm embraces Merriam Livingston-Vance asked, "How are you feeling?"

"Wonderful," said Keri as she fastened her gaze on the nearly-six foot woman with flaming red hair. Keri noticed every facial feature seemed to be in perfect proportion, as did her beautifully formed body. "I will admit though, I'm not looking forward to leaving. I feel so safe here."

"I understand," Merriam said, "but trust your instincts if a dangerous situation should occur, and if possible, control your fear."

Keri smiled. "Easy for you to say."

"We must leave now," Alexandria said, "the van is waiting."

***

The helicopter with Voger and Turnell on board set down in a clearing in Olympic National Park near two other choppers. Seven FBI agents were waiting nearby. Voger and Turnell were running toward them before the blades ceased whirling.

"A report!" yelled Voger.

Agent Harry Ford stepped forward, a large man in his forties with curly blonde hair, a cigar stub in his mouth. "At first light, or when this fog clears, we'll take another look at Shaw Island. We concentrated around the pavilion last night. This morning we'll search the other end."

Voger asked, "Where are the others?"

"Seattle, six in cars," Ford said. "Turnell said we should maintain surveillance at the docks, so we have men stationed at the ones where the ferries come in and at the major piers. We're also--"

The radio squawked and a voice said, "Is Turnell there yet?"

"Right here, who's on?"

"Kreps. Eric, did you get a plate number on that white Continental yesterday? "

Turnell thought for a moment. "Can't remember all of them but the first two numbers were three-seven. Why?"

"Well, I'm sitting here at Pier 52 and there are *two* white Continentals parked side by side nearby, one man in each one, like they're waiting for someone. No three-seven on the plates though."

Voger took the mike. "Back off, don't let them see you, and watch for any incoming boats. It may be just a coincidence with the cars, but you never know. If you see anything get on the radio fast. "

The large boat with enclosed seating areas for passengers was waiting at the dock as the van pulled up. "Let's hurry," Alexandria said. "It's going to be light soon. Fortunately the fog will give us ample cover until we reach land."

The four couples followed her on board and were barely in their seats when the powerful engines started and the boat moved forward into the open water.

"I've never been on a floating ship before," George Vance said, holding firmly to the arms of the seat.

"Then how did you get to the island?" Phillip asked. As soon as the question left his mouth he smiled. "Of course, I didn't think of that. None of you came here by normal transportation, right?"

Paula Ames, a medium height woman with short dark hair and gray eyes said, "Depends on the standard of normality. We're taking this little trip with you for the adventure of it, and you are correct in your assumption. When it was suggested we leave Washington and meet at our facility on the island, we simply *thought* our way here. We dematerialized our bodies and reappeared here in a matter of seconds."

Keri rolled her eyes. "My father will never believe me when I tell him about this. Neither will Chance Patton, my co-anchor at the station."

Robert Ames looked up. "Keri, did Chance Patton have a sister?"

"Yes, her name was Ruth. She died a few years ago."

Ames raised his eyebrows and looked at Carlton, then back at Keri. "I have to tell you your associate may be a part of Task Force Zero. Under hypnosis Patton's sister and Voger's mother both identified me as an alien. The two men must have initiated the plan to eliminate us."

He reached in his pocket, removed a cell phone and called the FBI headquarters in Washington. Knowing Director Brent was on his way to Seattle, he asked for either Assistant Director Gillespie or Agent Fowler. Fowler came on the line. Ames identified himself. "The person you're looking for at Channel Eleven isn't the news director. It's Chance Patton, Keri Winslow's co-anchor."

Fowler said he would bring Patton in for questioning and advised Ames that Director Brent's estimated time of arrival at the Bellevue residence was ten o'clock.

With the disconnect, Keri said, "I thought I knew him. I trusted him."

"People are not always what they seem to be," Ames said.

***

As the Falcon jet darted westward, Director Brent replaced the telephone and turned to his seat companion, Agent David Gasparri. "Getting the traffic choppers from the TV stations was a good idea. Thanks."

David nodded. "Voger's men will pay scant attention to what they would consider a normal occurrence."

"Let's *hope*," Brent said. "The Seattle-Tacoma airport reports no Bureau jet landing there this morning. Voger probably used a regional airport, fewer questions and less paperwork. I'm sure he is with his people now. Wish we had a tail wind."

***

The radio crackled, Kreps calling from Pier 59. "The fog's lifting and I can see a large boat coming this way."

"Get across the street and use your binoculars," Voger said. "I want a description of everyone getting off that boat."

In less than five minutes Kreps radioed back. "Okay, they're walking to the cars. There are...counting...nine of them. Wait a minute! Attorney General Ames is with them, Secretary Matthews too, and their wives. I believe the tall red-head is Ambassador Livingston-Vance."

Voger slapped his knee. "We've got them! Who else can you see?"

"There's a man I don't recognize. Must be the Ambassador's husband. And a young woman, a real beauty with long black hair halfway down her back, is walking in front. There's another couple, a good looking blonde woman, thirty-something, and the man with her is tall and slender with brown hair. They're getting into the car with the young brunette. The other six are all crowding into the second car."

Voger turned to Turnell. "Jesus Christ! The

blonde-haired woman with the man may be the Winslow woman with Phillip Lansing. You said--"

"It can't be her," Turnell said. It's another one of their people. Keri Winslow's dead. Trust me."

"You'd better be right!" He spoke again to Kreps. "Turnell and I will be in the air in minutes. I'm sending the other agents here back to Shaw Island. The rest of the aliens must still be there. As for you, follow the Continentals, but not too close. When they get where they're going call me. We'll find a place to land and you can pick us up. Alert your other men as to what's happening." He stared at Turnell. "And this time there won't be any mistakes."

Voger and Turnell lifted off with Agent Roy Palmer at the controls. "Stay close to the peninsula shoreline until we hear from Kreps," Voger said. Palmer nodded. The helicopter continued to make wide circles between Port Angeles and Port Townsend. Finally Kreps' voice was heard. "Damn, they split up, going opposite directions."

"Where are your men?" Voger screamed.

"They're on the way, should be... okay, I see Ruter's car now. Hold on." Kreps switched channels and told Ruter to follow the southbound vehicle, then back to Voger. "All right, we've got both of them covered. Stay open. We'll tell you when either car stops."

Voger let out a deep breath of frustration and called Ford on Shaw Island for a report. "No trace of anyone except an old woman at the dock," Ford said. Voger looked again at Turnell. "She said the ferry hadn't come in yet, and as far as she knew the island was deserted. We told her we were checking on a drug drop."

"Spread out and keep looking." After fifteen minutes he heard Kreps' voice.

"Voger, you're not going to believe this. The car Ruter was following, well--"

"Well what?"

"It stopped on the side of the road, and as Ruter slowed to pass it he couldn't see anyone inside."

"What?"

"That's right. So he pulled over and backed up to check it out. The car's empty. He can't figure out where they went."

Voger slammed his fist into the metal frame of the chopper. "Son of a bitch!" He shook his hand to ease the pain and said, "Where are you and the other car?"

"On Route 5 heading north, no idea where they're going. The traffic is very light. Maybe I should pull them over and--"

"No, stupid! Ford still can't find anyone on Shaw and there's a large group of those things still around. Maybe you're being led straight to them now. Don't arouse their suspicions. Let me know the minute they reach their destination."

***

"I thought we were going to Bellevue," Phillip said.

"We are," Alexandria said, "the long way, a

leisurely circle around Lake Washington so we can time our arrival in Bellevue with Director Brent's. We'll hit 405 in a bit and go back south."

"Where are the others?"

Alexandria grinned. "Taking an etheric stretch somewhere and doing some research. They aren't particularly fond of automobiles. We should all be in Bellevue at about the same time."

Phillip looked out the back window at the cars behind them. "What if we're being followed?"

Alexandria leaned back in the seat. "That would mean the timetable has been moved up and culmination will occur sooner than Director Brent planned."

Chapter 29

The pilot's voice on the intercom said, "Director Brent, you have a secured transmission coming in from Agent Blake, Seattle field office. You can take it on the desk phone."

Brent got up and went to the desk across the aisle, Gasparri following. "Yes, Ethan."

"Sir, one of my men in a traffic-report aircraft has spotted three FBI choppers on the ground at Shaw Island. He saw two men at the dock, one on the beach near the choppers. You said there were only fourteen of them. We're ready to go in when you give the word."

"Cancel the meeting at the airport and let's get this thing wrapped up. Get your team together and land near their choppers, fan out across that island and apprehend every one of them. The less firepower the better. These maniacs are going to stand trial. They've disgraced the Bureau."

"Mr. Director, if I might suggest, Agent Blake's unit should wear civilian clothes and use high-speed boats rather than choppers," David Gasparri said. "Voger's men will think they are pleasure seekers and will only attempt to wave them away. Four boats should be sufficient with two landing on the east side of the island to immobilize the agent on guard, disable the helicopters including the radios, and two boats going around to the west side. The men can then cut across land to link up with the others and make a closing circle."

"Ethan, did you hear that?" He held the phone so that Gasparri could listen.

"Yeah, but it might take us some time to--"

David took the phone. "Ethan, this is David Gasparri. You'll find the boats you need at Pier 69. The people there know me. Use my name and tell them it's a Bureau requisition. They'll understand." He handed the phone back to Brent.

"Get it done," the Director said, "and call me on my cell phone with updates of the situation before, during and after. We'll be landing in about half an hour and a car will be waiting to take us to Bellevue. Make sure the agents are placed in maximum security until we can take them back to Washington."

He replaced the phone and looked at David. "How do you know so much about the islands and Pier 69?"

"I grew up in Seattle, spent a lot of time on Shaw Island."

***

The large ranch-style house on the outskirts of Bellevue was situated on over an acre of tree-filled land. The Continental pulled into the driveway as Agent Kreps passed by. He immediately called Voger and gave him the address. "There's a school soccer field only a few miles from here near the intersection of Interstate 90 and Highway 405. I'll be waiting for you there."

"Call in Ruter and the others."

"I'll bring Ruter in but there were only four of them in the car, counting the driver. Two were women, so there's no problem. The other units are watching the airport."

"Bring them all in, and while you're waiting for us have them check the other houses in the neighborhood. I don't want anyone calling the local police when we make our move."

"I'll take care of it."

Voger tried to reach Agent Ford on Shaw Island for a report. No response on the radio.

***

Alexandria waved goodbye to the man in the white suit backing the car out of the driveway. She opened the back door to the house and Keri and Phillip followed her into the kitchen. "Fix yourselves something to eat if you're hungry. If not, just relax for awhile. Director Brent should be here soon to take you back to Washington. "

They walked into a long rectangular living room with the nearly thirty foot wall of floor to ceiling bookshelves, a rolling step ladder nearby. Phillip wasn't surprised to see the Matthews, Ames, and Vances perusing the books. He grinned. "Took a shortcut to the library, huh?"

"The only way to travel," Paula said. She walked over and took Keri's hand. "I was looking at a book on how the media shapes the world and thought about you two. I've watched you both on television many times, and I told the others that you'd make an excellent on-air team."

"Make that a team, period," Phillip said. "We're going to be married."

"Congratulations," Carlton said as the others applauded. "And Keri, I understand you will be working with Phillip on the book."

"We haven't talked about specific plans once this is over, but I would like to help in any way I can. First I have to see if I still have a job. "

Carlton looked at Alexandria and she nodded. "Phillip, to ease the burden I've made financial arrangements for you, and for Keri too, now that you're together." He handed him an envelope. "All the details are in there. A bank account in Washington has been set up for you. It represents what Eve and I have accumulated over the years, and we want you and Keri to have it."

"I don't know what to say."

"Think of it as a wedding present."

"The money will be wonderful," Keri said, "but I just suddenly realized we'll never see you or the others again."

Merriam Livingston-Vance embraced Keri. "You will someday." She turned to Alexandria. "While we were sans bodies this morning, we checked Tony Voger's records as you suggested."

Alexandria's laugh was rueful. "I'm sure what you found wasn't pleasant."

Phillip said, "What are you talking about?"

"The Akashic Records," Alexandria said. "They

represent primal energy in a force field where every action taken by each individual is impressed and recorded."

"Voger's made quite an impact," Robert Ames said. "He was responsible for the death of a man known as Alan Sorenson, a hypnotherapist, and for the murder of FBI agents who tried to defect Task Force Zero, although it was reported they were killed in a drug sting. Based on the continuity, the trend of his thoughts and beliefs, I see now how this whole matter can be resolved." Alexandria nodded.

"I don't understand," Phillip said, rubbing the stubble of a beard.

"Everyone's experience is based on his or her belief system," Carlton said. "In Voger's mind he is both a victim and an avenger. He is filled with fear and hatred and doesn't understand that what he does to others he does to himself. He is following a path of self-destruction."

"Keri, Phillip, excuse us," Alexandria said. She motioned to the Sigma group and they went into the bedroom and closed the door. Keri and Phillip were on the couch and almost asleep when Alexandria appeared beside them several minutes later.

"Conference over?" he asked.

"Yes. We have decided to be participants in Voger's experience as he continues on the path he has chosen. This will settle the matter in the most propitious way." She explained the plan and waited for their response. They both stared at her incredulously.

Finally Phillip said, "Then you think there will be a confrontation with Voger."

She nodded. "We feel it coming."

***

Following David Gasparri's plan to the letter, FBI agents under the command of Ethan Blake quickly immobilized the helicopters and had two of the rogue agents handcuffed and lying face down on the sandy beach. Another man from Blake's unit sprinted toward the dock while the others spread out and began moving in a half-circle to meet the agents coming across from the west side.

Allowing sufficient time for the men to get into position, Agent Blake crouched low in the dense forest and used a bullhorn: "Voger, or whoever is in charge here, listen to me. There's no way out. Your choppers are inoperative you are surrounded on all sides. Your only alternative is to surrender peacefully. Raise your weapons high and start walking toward the beach where you came in."

A shot cut into a tree near Blake, followed by automatic fire and a distant groan. "Man down!" Blake recognized Harry Ford's voice. Blake slid on his belly in that direction until he could see two men in a clearing, one on the ground, the other examining him.

"No sudden moves," Blake said as he stood up, automatic rifle in hand. "Very carefully now, drop your weapons and kick them over here."

An agent who had slipped up behind the two men said, "Do as he says."

Agent Ford tossed the guns toward Blake. "Ty's been hit, leg wound. He needs help."

"He'll get it as soon as the rest of your men throw it in. It's all over, Ford. We outnumber you. The fight's over. Let it go or we'll have no choice but to take you all back in body bags." He pitched him the bullhorn. "Tell them, Ford, *now!*"

Ford repeated the message, picked up the wounded agent and began walking toward the beach. Within minutes the other three renegade agents emerged from the trees, hands up, weapons high.

Blake said, "We've got two on the beach. Where are the rest of them? There are supposed to be fourteen."

"There are only seven of us," Ford said. "Turnell is with Voger in a chopper. The others are on the mainland."

Agent Blake pulled out his cell phone and made a call.

Chapter 30

Keri had stepped into the kitchen for a glass of water. Hearing her scream Phillip bounced off the couch, but before he could reach the kitchen Tony Voger came through the door, his left arm around Keri's neck, a gun in his right hand pointed at her temple. "This lady was supposed to be dead and buried and I'll make sure it happens this time." Keri's eyes were wide as Voger led her into the room, several men behind him armed with automatic weapons.

Phillip said, "You must be Tony Voger, *formerly* of the FBI. And which one of you is Turnell?" Turnell didn't answer. "Well, never mind. As the saying goes, gentlemen, we finally have you where we want you."

Voger's eyes flashed. "You're sick." He turned to his men. "Check every room, and see if there's an attic. If you find anyone you know what to do. You stay with me Turnell, and make sure Lansing's not carrying anything."

Turnell walked to Phillip, turned him around and raised his arms. The frisk produced nothing.

Voger said, "All right, Lansing, tell me where those creatures are hiding or Winslow is the first to go. Makes no difference to me."

Turnell said, "Tony, let's think this out. No one's been killed yet and maybe we could--"

"You fool! You *stupid* fool!" He pressed the gun

barrel against Keri's head. "I've risked everything to bring these people to justice, and as far as I'm concerned this woman and Lansing are of the same ilk. So don't cross me, Turnell, or you'll be joining them."

Keri remembered Merriam's words...*trust your instincts...control your fear.* She saw deep sorrow in Turnell's eyes as their gaze met, then a slight motion of his hand, an almost imperceptible movement upward as he looked at Voger. She could see the loathing he felt for him, knew what he was going to do, draw his gun and kill him. She took a sudden short breath and went limp, breaking loose from Voger's grasp, slipping to the floor. Phillip moved quickly to cover her.

Voger was jarred off balance, but was able to fire before Turnell's gun was out of the holster, the bullet hitting him in the left arm. He spun around and fell on the couch. "I've got another one for you, you traitorous son of a bitch," Voger said as he removed Turnell's gun. "But I'll let you bleed a little first."

Keri opened her eyes for a second, winked at Phillip. He realized she had faked the faint. He stood up as the other agents came running into the room.

Seeing Turnell wounded and Keri on the floor, Kreps asked, "Who did this?"

"I did," Voger said. "He was having second thoughts. The woman just fainted"

Phillip said, "Look Voger, you're after the aliens. Don't lose sight of what you came to do. I know where they are."

Before Voger could speak, the door to the

bedroom opened and Robert Ames walked out and the agents raised their guns.

"I checked that room," Ruter said. "No one was in there."

Phillip was stunned to see the entourage following behind Ames, not only Alexandria and the three couples, but all of the other missing twelve and their spouses. He couldn't remember the names of some of the wives and husbands, but he recognized most of them: Admiral Frank Jessops and his wife Elizabeth, Senator Burton Obrey and Helen, Senator Lisa Cluse and husband Ted, General and Mrs. Frederick Craig, Chief Justice and Mrs. Simon Ellenberg, House Speaker Julius Andrews and his wife Megan, Senator Claudia Ferguson and husband Paul, Senator and Mrs. Curtis O'Connor, and Senator and Mrs. Jason Miller.

Phillip noticed the agents backing away and crowding around Voger. Turnell remained on the couch. Keri got up and leaned against the wall.

"Well I'll be damned," Voger said, "the twenty-four I've been tracking. Check them for weapons." As his men began the search, Voger walked over to face Robert Ames. "And here is Mr. Attorney General himself, 'one of us' said the monster who killed my mother. Is that right Ames? A lizard from some slimy swamp on another planet disguised as one of us? I'd like to see what you really look like before I blow you away."

Ames said, "As expressions of God, there is no difference in the two of us."

Voger laughed. "Yeah, sure." He patted Ames' chest with his gun. "I wonder if you have a heart. Let's see." He leveled the gun and fired. Ames looked at him for a second, fell to the floor. Phillip started to move toward him but felt the barrel of a rifle in his back.

Keep an eye on all of them," Voger said as he moved to where Alexandria was standing. "And this dark haired beauty is an extra-added attraction. What's your name, honey?"

"Alexandria," she said, a smile on her lips, eyes shining.

"Are you one of them?"

"Oh yes! And so are you."

He raised the gun, pressing it hard into her stomach. "Don't you wish." He pulled the trigger and her head jerked back.

Their eyes met, and she said softly, "I forgive you." His face twitched and he stepped back and fired again. Her eyes slowly closed and she dropped to the floor.

Keri turned around and faced the wall, her hands on her head. Phillip was quickly beside her. "I think I'm going to be sick," she said.

Voger said, "All of you...spread out in front of that wall of books."

"What about these two?" Kreps asked, pointing to Keri and Phillip.

"I'll leave them for Turnell. He can finish the job, or I'll finish him."

Voger took an automatic weapon from one of his

men and went to the opposite side of the room. "We bless you," Paula Ames said. He gave a smirk and began firing, bullets raking across the men and women at chest level, each body recoiling back and falling. When it was over, twenty-five bodies were on the floor of the large living room.

Chapter 31

Voger motioned for Turnell. "If you haven't lost too much blood, the last two are yours."

"I don't think so," Director Brent said. He had entered through the back of the house just as the fusillade was over. Standing near the doorway of the kitchen, he saw only Alexandria's body, and the shock on Voger's face. Agents Blake and York were beside Brent with guns in hand, David Gasparri coming through the front door with other agents. His "drop your weapons *now*" resounded through the room and the command was quietly obeyed.

Brent moved into the room and saw Robert Ames and the other bodies crumpled in front of the bookcase. He screamed, "My God, Voger, what have you done? Oh, Jesus! It's all of them...you killed them *all*."

As the director looked at each body, Voger staring at the ceiling, Keri hurried to where Turnell was sitting, his hand gripping his arm to slow the bleeding. She said, "If Alexandria could forgive Voger, I can certainly forgive you."

He closed his eyes, his head shaking, questioning. "I don't know how you can. I thought I'd killed you." He looked up. "Flesh wound?"

She nodded. "You did what you thought you had to do, but I could tell it was difficult for you. And I'm not going to testify against you, not after you risked your life to save us."

His eyes closed again. "I was afraid of Voger, guess that's why I didn't act fast enough. Now it's hard to believe I was even a part of this carnage."

She touched his hand. "You weren't."

Phillip said, "Mr. Director, I'm Phillip Lansing and that's Keri Winslow. We witnessed everything."

Brent glanced at them and back at Voger. "May God help you!" He removed his handkerchief and covered his mouth, the reality of the massacre beginning to affect his stomach. "A goddamn blood bath! Why, Voger, *why*?"

"An eye for an eye, and I'd do it again. You'll understand when I explain everything to you."

"Blake, cuff these so-called *agents* and get them out of my sight, and call your office and get a van over here to haul them away. And Gasparri, contact the local authorities. Tell them to bring the medical examiner."

Phillip whispered to Gasparri, "Don't call the police yet. I need to talk to Director Brent." Gasparri nodded. Phillip waited until Voger and his men had been taken outside, and said, "Director Brent, may we speak to you alone?"

Brent motioned for the other agents to leave the room, said, "At least we got here in time to save you and Winslow. I don't imagine Voger would leave any witnesses." He coughed. "I just wish we could have gotten here sooner."

Keri said, "Director Brent, Eric Turnell tried to stop Voger and was wounded in the process. I think he should be given some special consideration."

"Didn't he try to kill you on the island?"

"I'm still here and my testimony wouldn't be what some prosecutor would be looking for."

Brent sighed. "He'll still be charged with conspiracy to commit murder."

Phillip said, "Mr. Director, what are you going to tell the president?"

"The truth, that the missing twelve and their wives and husbands were gunned down by Tony Voger working with a clandestine group of FBI agents. Robert Ames explained to me why they were after them, something to do with their association with a deep-cover terrorist group."

"You can say Voger *thought* there was such a connection. In truth, they really had nothing to do with anything even closely related to such a group. These were innocent people."

"I'll make that clear."

Phillip hesitated. "Now that Tony Voger will get what he deserves, and President Underwood can explain to the press and the nation why the missing people won't be returning, I think we're ready for the final act of this scenario. And I know, Mr. Director, you will keep what you are about to see in confidence."

There was a puzzled look on Brent's face. "What are you talking about?"

"Look behind you."

As Brent turned around, Alexandria stood up, the bullet holes in her dress clearly visible. Then the others opened their eyes and were soon on their feet. As Robert Ames walked toward Brent, the Director's face became ashen, eyes wide, a look of horror on his face.

"It's all right," Robert said, "nothing to fear." He opened his shirt to show smooth skin without a scratch.

Brent found a chair and sat down. He looked at Phillip. "I don't understand."

The beautiful woman with the Eurasian eyes said, "Mr. Director, my name is Alexandria, and we played a role on your stage of life to enable cosmic law to take its course. Voger did temporarily extinguish our physical systems. From your human perspective, he shot and killed us."

Brent tried to swallow but couldn't, his mouth dry.

Keri said, "I was as shocked as you are now when I was told who these people are. They are from another universe."

He whispered, "My wife was right...the coded message...you're from Sirius."

Alexandria smiled. "She was close. Director Brent, our bodies are materialized thought-forms which can be damaged but quickly healed by our minds, and this is something all of you will learn someday. But earthlings aren't the only ones unaware of this ancient discipline. Even some of the people in the lower dimensions of our world are not fully capable of immediate restoration and may at times leave their bodies on this plane." She smiled. "Of course, certain officials of your government are aware of this. I'm referring to the Roswell incident in nineteen forty-seven and the removal of the bodies. I believe they were taken to a CIA warehouse in Langley, Virginia."

"I don't know anything about that."

"Startling revelations will soon be made, Mr. Director. It is time the world knows the truth."

There was a pleading look on his face. "But what am I going to tell my agents?"

"Take Voger and his men away," Alexandria said. "Let your agents leave without coming back in here. They will assume the local police have been called, the bodies to be taken to the morgue."

"I don't know what kind of a case we can present against Voger without evidence of the killings."

Suddenly a shot rang out behind the house. Brent got up and ran to the door, Phillip and Keri behind him. "What happened?"

Someone hollered, "Voger killed himself." Agent Blake ran to the back steps. "York removed Voger's cuffs so he could urinate. There was a scuffle for York's weapon...Voger got it and put the barrel in his mouth. God, Chief, it happened so fast. I'm sorry."

"Tell York he won't be disciplined for his carelessness," the director said. "It was the play's final curtain."

"What was that last part?" Blake asked.

"Never mind." Noticing the FBI van pulling up, he said, "I don't want to wait for the Seattle cops. Take him downtown with his men. Maybe it'll give them time to think about what happens to vigilantes. I'll be along soon, want to get a full statement from Lansing and

Winslow." He closed the screen door and returned to the living room.

He started to relay the information about Voger's death, but Robert Ames said, "We heard." He pointed to a large manila envelope on the mantel. "We didn't know exactly where Voger's mind would take him, but just in case we have provided you with the details of three murders he committed--time, place, witnesses, and other pertinent evidence. Take the material with you for the files."

Brent wiped his brow. "What happens now?"

"We're going home," Robert Ames said, "back to our world. We will simply disappear without a trace, as we did in Washington."

"How do you do that?"

Ames smiled. "I understand your curiosity. Wallace, the instability of the proton, the subatomic particles at the center of atoms, is the key. To disappear we use our minds to increase the vibration of protons to the point of disintegration, which causes matter to evaporate into radiation. To appear we simply reverse the process."

The director shook his head. "But why were you here on earth?"

"Our mission has to do with the healing of the mass mind of humanity, and part of the plan was to initiate the communications revolution. The Internet as a dynamic force-field in space has now accelerated the mind-energy of the collective consciousness, which will soon undergo a massive shift and bring forth a transition from the old world to the new. The truth will then be understood."

The director appeared bewildered. "What are you saying?"

"It is through global communications that the citizens of your world will find unity, and through this harmonious cooperation concepts of race and religion will change dramatically. As people understand the true meaning of oneness, they will forgive one another and cease fearful actions leading to guilt and punishment. Our assignment is to help in that process. In time you will understand everything." Ames extended his hand. "Thank you, Wallace. It was a privilege and pleasure knowing you."

Brent shook his hand. "I've always thought of myself as fairly open minded, but I could not have been prepared for what I've seen and heard here today. And I won't say anything. No one will believe me anyway."

"It will all come out," Ames said, "but *your* knowledge of the truth of us, of everyone, will not be revealed unless it is your choice. Now we must go." He stepped back and the twenty-five people of the Sigma group from a galactic cluster parallel to Sirius in the constellation Canis Major joined hands.

"Wait," Phillip said. He rushed over to Carlton and embraced him, then kissed Eve gently on the lips. He said, "Thank you for being my friends."

They smiled and Eve said, "We love you, Phillip."

"Till we meet again," Carlton said.

Keri had begun at the other end and was moving

down the line, touching each one's face, further expressing her feelings in words. When she reached the last one, Alexandria, she asked, "We'll see you again, won't we, I mean in this life?"

Alexandria whispered, "Yes, we have some unfinished business." She raised her voice. "Now both of you stand back over there with Director Brent, and please turn around and close your eyes. The intense illumination could blind you for a moment."

There was a soft whooshing sound, and when they turned back seconds later the living room was empty. "They're home," Phillip said. There were tears in his eyes.

Chapter 32

At the televised press conference, FBI Director Wallace Brent was standing to the left and slightly behind President Samual Underwood. The camera framed a head and shoulder shot, the President was cued and he began speaking, a slow and deliberate address to the American people informing them of Brent's discovery of the bullet-ridden bodies of twelve of our nation's leaders along with their wives and husbands. He revealed that Tony Voger, a Special Agent of the FBI, had fired the shots.

"Agent Voger thought they were allied with a deep-cover terrorist group, and he considered his actions in the interest of national security," the president said. "However, it has been proven conclusively the officials were not in any way connected with such a group. They had left the city together only because they were alerted by a loyal FBI agent that their lives were in danger. Agent Voger committed suicide as he was taken into custody."

The president reported that the other agents accompanying Voger as part of an unsanctioned covert operation called Task Force Zero had been arrested. When he completed his summary, the flurry of questions in the press room began.

Roland of AP asked, "Mr. President, where did the shootings take place?"

"In a private home in Seattle. I can't tell you more because we want to protect the privacy of the owner who was out of the city at the time."

The bearded correspondent for CNN asked, "Which deep-cover terrorist group are you referring to?"

"We have a name, but there is no mention of them in the files of the intelligence community. We're still checking."

The plump short-haired woman from Fox News asked, "Who identified the bodies and where have they been taken?"

"Director Brent made the identifications." The president hesitated. "They have since been returned home to closest next of kin. A memorial service for all twenty-four will be held in the Capitol Rotunda on Friday."

A reporter wearing sun glasses identified himself as being with the *Washington Post*, said, "We understand one of the anchors with Channel Eleven here in Washington was arrested and charged with conspiracy in this matter. Any truth to that?"

The president looked at Director Brent. He stepped forward and said, "A man from that station was brought in for questioning and was later released. It was determined he called the FBI to report on a possible lead to the missing people, but there is only a circumstantial connection between him and Task Force Zero." What the Director didn't say was that Chance Patton had quit his job and left town. His whereabouts were unknown. The FBI was not pursuing him.

The president pointed to a raised hand. It was the new White House correspondent for CBC, a tall thin man wearing a pin-stripped suit. "Mr. President, have you thought about who will fill the positions vacated by the deaths of the twelve?"

President Underwood read from a paper naming those who would complete the terms of the six congressional seats and his short list for a new Justice of the Supreme Court, Secretary of State, Attorney General, two Joint Chiefs, and the Ambassador to the United Nations.

A reporter from the *New York Times* asked if she could pose a question to Director Brent. The president nodded.

She smiled. "Mr. Director, we've heard about Agent Harry Ford's insistence that the undercover group had been following those people thinking they were aliens from another planet, and that Voger killed them as a service to the country. Can you add anything to that?"

There was laughter in the room and Brent waited until they were quiet. He said, "No, I can't, and I would hope that you in here won't either. In my opinion, Agent Voger was insane and his insanity killed him. That's all I have to say."

Press Secretary Harley took over, and President Underwood and FBI Director Brent quickly left the room.

Chapter 33

Keri submitted her resignation the day after going on-air to report on President Underwood's press conference, offering no personal comments relating to the experience. She and Phillip were married in Charlottesville a week later, her father and Phillip's parents in attendance with several close friends. Within the month they found their perfect home in the Blue Ridge Mountains and moved in during the last days of winter.

"We're going to enjoy it here," Keri said as she unpacked a box in Phillip's study. "No close neighbors, a good place to write."

Phillip was sitting on the floor looking at the pages Alexandria had given him. "I agree. Since everything has settled down maybe I can do some work on the book."

Keri put her hair back into a ponytail, said, "Tomorrow is soon enough." She took his hand. "Come on, let's take a walk. The sun has broken through the clouds and it's a beautiful day." She slipped on a jacket and they walked outside. She asked, "Do you think we'll hear from Director Brent again?"

"Maybe one of these days. I think we answered most of his questions on the plane ride back to Washington. He made copious notes, said they were for his wife, Millie, that her mother and grandfather had always believed in life 'out there', and she grew up with total acceptance of it. But I don't think they'll be doing much talking about the Sigma group."

They climbed a gentle rolling hill and looked back at their colonial home nestled in the trees below, a large white swing on the front porch. Suddenly it started moving back and forth as though being pushed forcefully by unseen hands. "Do you see what I see?" Keri asked.

"Uh huh, and there's no wind."

"Do you think--?"

Before she could finish the question, Alexandria materialized on the swing dressed in sweater and jeans, her long black hair glistening in the sunlight. She smiled and waved. Phillip and Keri ran toward her, and she came to meet them, arms wide for an embrace.

"Hi, dear ones," she said, "thought I'd drop in for a surprise visit."

They hugged her and Phillip said with a grin, "We've got to stop meeting like this. People might talk."

"Yeah," Keri said, "if they saw the way you zapped in here we'd be the gossip of the mountain folk. Come on in and I'll show you around and fix some tea."

"Beautiful setting," Alexandria said as they walked toward the house arm in arm. "I think you picked the perfect spot for your work." She looked at Phillip. "You know this book won't be your last one on this subject. If you need any help here's the number where you can reach me. The call goes through a special relay bypassing the regular system, but is activated by any telephone."

Phillip took the slip of paper. "To be honest with you, I haven't written a page since we left the island, but I do have a pretty good outline. Director Brent told us on the plane about his meeting at the White House right after the disappearances. That's my beginning, change of names of course, and Keri gave me a detailed rundown of what happened at the TV station, her conversation with Chance Patton and the bartender who talked about the supposed antimatter device. I'm also going to plug in what she remembers about the morning Senator Obrey's car was found." He paused on the front porch. "Alexandria, I'm thinking about making it a novel. Any objections?"

"No, not at all. The seeds will be sown even if the reader considers it all fiction."

Phillip opened the door, and Keri took Alexandria's hand. "We couldn't have had such a beautiful home without the help of Carlton and Eve. Let me give you a quick tour while Phillip makes the tea."

***

As the three settled in the living room, Phillip continued with his outline. "I'm going to recount Carlton's phone call and the trip to Seattle through both my perspective and Keri's, and take us all the way through what happened at the house in Bellevue."

"You know," Alexandria said, "people will think your story is based on a wildly imaginative account of the missing officials and their demise." Phillip nodded. "Even so, I agree with you that it's the best way to handle the story. It will be believed on some level of consciousness, and that's what counts."

Keri refilled the cups. "I'm beginning to realize what a strange world this is. When you have something important to say, something that could change lives and help people find true joy and peace, few listen and still fewer believe."

"That's changing," Alexandria said, a bemused look on her face.

Phillip said, "You mentioned that there were about a hundred million interdimensionals on earth at this time in human form. How many are in the U.S.?"

"Close to five million. They are spread all over the country in cities and towns, active in a variety of ways to assist in the transformation. Only a small percentage are currently in government service."

"I didn't look for any distinguishable characteristics when we were with the group," Keri said. "Is there a way to spot the Sigma people?"

Alexandria smiled. "Only if you look closely. For one thing, our palms have few lines. There's also much light emanating from our eyes. I'm sure you've recognized that. And if you noticed back on the island and in Bellevue, we maintain longer eye contact than is generally accepted by people here. We seldom blink, and the fastened gaze can sometimes be disconcerting."

Phillip thought about Carlton, said, "I would also add a strong sense of composure. I can't remember Carlton being nervous, impatient, or overly excited about anything. He was always self-assured and displayed great poise in every situation."

"But don't forget," Alexandria said, "we can play a role when necessary."

"I'll never forget," Keri said softly.

"Something else I wanted to ask you about," Phillip said. "In those pages you typed for me, you talked about the great shift in the collective unconscious that is coming."

"Yes, and to the pockets of resistance it will be the terrible times." She smiled. "But for the majority of people on the planet it will be a time of great rejoicing. War, holy or not, will be considered imbecilic. Gone will be the days of religious perversion, jingoism, fear-based initiatives by government and erosions of personal freedom."

"The Sigma group has already helped the country move in that direction," Phillip said. "I'm sure they influenced President Underwood in many of his decisions."

"His actions were his own originality."

"When will the major shift in consciousness take place?" Keri asked.

"That's one reason I stopped by. We want the book released as quickly as possible. The publisher is waiting for your manuscript, so let it be your top priority."

"We'll get right on it," Phillip said.

"To answer your question, Keri, the shift will begin in the year twenty twenty-five."

"That's only three years away," Phillip said.

"Yes, and that is why it is important you and Keri

help us to prepare the people." She paused for a moment. "First there must be a World Declaration of Independence and a World Bill of Rights, then the stage will be set for a new world economy based on right human relations. The shift will be hardly noticeable at first, except for those who are in tune with their intuitive powers. But when it is completed there will be a series of events resulting in the greatest outpouring of love the world has ever seen. It is through this energy of love the final transformation will be made."

She walked over and took Keri's hand. "Speaking of love, Mrs. Lansing, how's married life?"

Realizing Alexandria wanted to change the subject, Keri said, "I never knew I could be so happy. It's a dream come true."

"I feel the same way," Phillip said. "I didn't know I could love someone like this."

Alexandria said, "Only those who have moved past ego domination can find true love because the defected personality does not understand love. According to an ancient teaching, find one person in the world you can love without judgment, one person whom you can see as completely innocent, and you will awaken to your truth of being. I believe you're doing that."

Keri smiled. "Alexandria, back on the island you told me about *nweering*, remember?"

"Yes," Alexandria said, "a rapturous interfusion of twin energies."

Keri noticed Phillip's puzzled expression. "Well, I

think I've found the complementary part of myself, my energy equivalent. Our energies seem to harmonize beautifully, *ecstatically*."

Alexandria flashed a broad smile. "What I think you're trying to say, Keri, is that you have finally met your match."

Chapter 34

Thomas Waters, a partner in one of Houston's largest law firms, picked up the ringing telephone on his desk. It was his private line. "Yes?" He heard the voice on the other end and said, "Good to hear from you."

"Tom, I've contacted the eleven, and they're ready to come aboard. Now with you as attorney general the team is complete. I want to call a press conference and announce the new appointments as soon as possible. When can you come to Washington?"

"I've wrapped up everything here and I'll leave today, if that meets with your approval."

President Samual Underwood said, "You and Stephanie come to Camp David on Saturday. I'll call the others. We'll spend the weekend together finalizing our plans."

"Transportation?"

"Take a plane and call me with your time of arrival. I'll have a car pick you up. Too many secret service agents around for our way of travel."

"I understand."

"Oh, I've added five more to our strategic policy team. I'm naming one of us to head up the CIA, and we'll also have a new Secretary of Defense, Treasury Secretary, National Security Advisor, and White House Chief of Staff."

"That makes seventeen," Waters said. "With you,

eighteen. Sigma. Significant, don't you think?"

"I would say so."

***

As spring turned to summer, Phillip worked on the manuscript and clipped numerous news items from the papers:

Population explosion dramatically slows-- *The Washington Post*

Denominationalism seen crumbling in America with new fellowship in religion--*Houston Chronicle*

Sharp reduction in crime, accidents and 911 calls attributed to sun spot activity--*New York Times*

Occupancy rates for area hospitals decline by sixty percent--*Los Angeles Times*

He leafed through the other articles on record high employment, the booming economy and rising income, the discovery of new supplies of food and energy and surpluses of earthly resources, dramatic reduction of airborne pollutants, and a healthier ecosystem. Phillip smiled. He knew he was seeing signs of the Sigma program. In September he watched the president's televised remarks to foreign journalists.

The speech was billed as Underwood's response to clamors in the European community for a one-world government. He addressed that issue by saying that conformity to any particular political ideology should not be an international goal, that a uniform government is not yet practical because of the different cultures and traditions of nations.

"However," he said, *"before I leave you tonight I want to tell you what I see for our global future. We are moving quickly toward a new world economy based on right human relations. The hold on the world's resources by international financiers will soon be broken and the banking and financial institutions known today will give way to a completely new structure incorporating social responsibility, human rights, and spiritual values.*

"Money will be directed from materialistic and selfish ends and focused on planetary healing and the constructive renewal of society. We are moving into an era of cooperative capitalism where the means of production and distribution will continue to be privately owned, but there will be less government control because the management of wealth and resources will be returned to the people. In the satisfaction of material needs the emphasis will be placed on working for the common purpose of the world, for the mutual benefit of all, as global consciousness replaces selfish interests.

"I want to issue the call tonight for a World Declaration of Independence and a World Bill of Rights. And I want to see a decentralization of power everywhere brought about by the clear thinking of people rather than governments, the deeming appropriateness of violence and exploitation giving way to a recognition of a one-world common interest. It is time."

After the president made his concluding remarks, Phillip turned to Keri. "Could he possibly be one of them?"

"If he's not, Alexandria is his speech writer." She walked to the phone and dialed the twelve digit number.

In response to Keri's question, Alexandria said, "I'll call you back in the morning."

***

A week later Phillip and Keri were warmly greeted in the Oval Office by the President of the United States and First Lady Julia.

After a few minutes of mundane conversation about weather, the Redskins, and if Phillip and Keri missed television reporting, Phillip said, "Mr. President, we were just guessing when we called Alexandria after watching your televised address. Since you invited us to the White House, we're assuming you're not concerned we know the truth about you."

"I don't think people will seriously consider the possibility that aliens are running this government," Julia Underwood said.

"We agree," Keri said, "but just to make sure, we're writing the book as a novel bordering on science fiction. We wouldn't want to do or say anything that would compromise your mission."

"We know," the president said, "and that's why we consider you and Phillip the first and only honorary members of the Sigma group. We trust you. However, I must tell you that when Alexandria called, our first consideration was to have you maintain your distance from official Washington." He laughed. "We didn't want the public to start wondering if you had insider information."

"While we want to bring about a changing of minds." Julia said, "we didn't want people looking in this direction with suspicious eyes."

"But after thinking about it," the president said, "we don't believe there is any reason for concern. Since it will be a fictional work, most people will see the book as strictly of your imagination, an outlandish story based on the disappearances of certain government officials. Others may resonate with the information that Alexandria has given you and begin to open their minds and hearts to a higher reality. That was the primary reason Carlton wanted you to write the book."

"To sow the seeds is the way Alexandria put it," Phillip said.

"And a mighty harvest will be reaped," the president said.

Phillip cleared his throat. "Mr. President, did the original twelve know you were one of them from the very beginning?"

Underwood smiled. "Yes, but we didn't come in together. I followed about six months later. The plan was for me to enter alone and not associate with any of what we called the strategic policy team, the twelve. We can see now that this was a wise move because I could have easily been on Tony Voger's list if I was suspected as being a part of the group. We had not counted on Jim Morris not finishing his term in office." He paused and glanced at the ceiling. "I know they wanted to complete what they came to do. I wish they could have. I miss them."

Keri said, "Mr. President, having known three of the couples fairly well, and now you and Mrs. Underwood, I feel I have been given a precious gift. I am eternally grateful. Thank you both for your confidence in Phillip and me."

The president stood and walked around the desk. "Being associated with us is just a continuation of what began long ago. Keri, do you remember Tom and Stephanie Waters?"

"Yes, they lived next door to us in Charlottesville for a time, and I read he was appointed attorney general. Wait a minute, you don't mean--"

"Yes, he and Stephanie are a part of Sigma. I've invited them to have a private dinner with the four of us this evening. It was Tom who called Randall Erickson and recommended you for the job with WTCX-TV here in Washington, and you've met others of us along the way."

"My God, I didn't know."

"And of course, Phillip, you and Carlton Matthews became good friends, and as with Keri, there have been other Sigma people who have been helpful to you since childhood."

"What Sam is trying to say," Julia said, "is that you just never know when you might be rubbing elbows with one of us. We are in the corporate world and small businesses, the churches, Wall Street, science, publishing, the media, arts and entertainment, everywhere. We're very good at playing roles to escape detection."

"But you do have a few distinguishable features if people know what to look for," Keri said. "Alexandria told us about them." She turned to look into Phillip's shining eyes and held the gaze. He didn't blink. She took a deep breath, quickly took his hand and looked at the palm. "Just wanted to make sure," she said with a nervous laugh.

The beginning

About the Author

John Randolph Price is an internationally known author and lecturer. Formerly a CEO in the corporate world, he has devoted over 40 years to researching the universal mysteries and ancient wisdom, and incorporating this fact-finding in the writing of numerous books.

John and his wife, Jan, originated World Healing Day that began on December 31, 1986, with over 500-million participants and has continued each year on the same date. His work has earned national and international awards for humanitarianism, progress toward global peace, and contributing to a higher degree of positive living in this world.